SCHOLASTIC
ENGLISH SKILL

CW00540901

Spelling and vocabulary
Year 6

Author
Shelley Welsh

Editorial
Rachel Morgan, Anna Hall,
Emily Anderson and
Red Door Media

Series design
Shelley Best and Anna Oliwa

Design team
Nicolle Thomas and Andrea Lewis

Illustrations
Dave Shepherd/The Bright Agency

**CD-ROM design and
development team**
Hannah Barnett, Phil Crothers and
MWA Technologies Private Ltd

Scholastic Education, an imprint of Scholastic Ltd
Book End, Range Road, Witney, Oxfordshire, OX29 0YD
Registered office: Westfield Road, Southam,
Warwickshire CV47 0RA
www.scholastic.co.uk

Printed and bound by Ashford Colour Press
© 2016 Scholastic Ltd
1 2 3 4 5 6 7 8 9   6 7 8 9 0 1 2 3 4 5

British Library Cataloguing-in-Publication Data
A catalogue record for this book is available from
the British Library.
ISBN 978-1407-14187-9

Extracts from The National Curriculum for England, English Programme of Study © Crown Copyright. Reproduced under the terms of the Open Government Licence (OGL). www.nationalarchives. gov.uk/doc/open-government-licence/version/3/

Every effort has been made to trace copyright holders for the works reproduced in this book, and the publishers apologise for any inadvertent omissions.

Contents

Chapter 1
Revisit and reinforce

Chapter 2
Suffixes

Chapter 3
Spelling patterns and letter strings

Chapter 4
Word families, roots and origins

Chapter 5
Tricky words

Chapter 6
Improving your work

Introduction

Scholastic English Skills: Spelling and vocabulary

Learning to spell depends on much more than simply memorising words. Exercises, word lists and tests are not enough. Children need to actively engage in the process, tackling new words using knowledge and skills acquired, taking risks and making errors. Purposeful writing is a key to learning to spell. Children need to see spelling as a useful tool for communication (rather than a rod to be beaten with!). To study the spelling of words we need to take them out of context but context is needed to learn how to use them and to give purpose for using them. Children need to know more than just how to spell words, they need to know what they mean as well, as such spelling and vocabulary are intrinsically linked.

This series provides a bank of adaptable ideas and resources for teaching spelling and vocabulary. Each chapter is, to some extent, independent of the others and chapters do not, therefore, always need to be followed in order. Activities within a section sometimes build upon each other and should be followed sequentially. It is anticipated that sections and activities will be selected as required to fit in with medium-term planning for each term.

Overview of the teaching of spelling and vocabulary

In English the relationship between sounds and letters (phonics) has been complicated by the complex history of the English language and there is not a simple one-to-one correspondence. Despite this complexity, a great deal of the relationship between letters and sounds is rule-bound, which means phonics works, but not all of the time. There is logic and pattern but there are also 'oddities'.

However spelling does not only represent sound; it also represents grammar and meaning. For example, the 'ed' suffix that identifies regular past-tense verbs can be pronounced 'd' or 'id' or 't' but never 'ed', but it is always spelled 'ed'. If spelling only represented sound, different accents would require different spellings. Instead of viewing the complexity as a problem, perhaps we might more usefully celebrate the richness and resourcefulness of English spelling.

Teaching spelling involves drawing children's attention to patterns: patterns of sounds and letters, patterns related to grammatical functions and patterns related to word origin. Although English spelling does have 'rules', such as 'q' is always followed by 'u', it is much more realistic to talk about patterns, conventions, possibilities and probabilities. Many so-called rules have so many exceptions or are so complex to explain, that they are not worth teaching. To teach something as a rule which is later contradicted is not helpful. Children become active, constructive learners by investigating and generalising common patterns, and acknowledging exceptions.

Vocabulary can be developed indirectly when children engage daily in oral language, listen to adults read to them and read extensively on their own. Vocabulary should also be taught directly both as individual words and word-learning strategies. Children need to develop curiosity about words and meanings. Good vocabulary teaching involves active engagement and fosters excitement about words, which leads to children attending more closely to them.

About the product

This book contains activities for teaching spelling and vocabulary. Each chapter focuses on a different aspect of spelling knowledge or skills and is divided into sections. Each section includes teachers' notes – objective, background knowledge, notes on how to use the photocopiable pages, further ideas and digital content – and three photocopiable pages. Each chapter also features a poster and assessment section. At the end of the book you will find a glossary of terms, a word bank providing banks of words to be used in games and other activities, and general activities which provides a set of generic games, activities and circle times linked to the activities in this book.

Posters

Each chapter has one poster. These posters are related to the content of the chapter and should be displayed and used for reference throughout the work on the chapter. The poster notes (on the chapter opening page) offer suggestions for how they could be used. There are black and white versions in the book and full-colour versions on the CD-ROM for you to print out or display on your whiteboard.

Assessment

Each chapter concludes with an assessment section. It summarises the curriculum objectives and activities in the section, provides pointers on observation and record keeping and includes one assessment photocopiable page.

Activities

Each section contains photocopiable page activities in the book. Each photocopiable page is also included on the CD-ROM for you to display or print out (answers are also provided, where appropriate, in a separate document on the CD-ROM).

Many of the photocopiable pages have linked interactive activities on the CD-ROM. These interactive activities are designed to act as starter activities to the lesson, giving whole-class support on the information being taught. However, they can also work equally well as plenary activities, reviewing the work the children have just completed.

Workbooks

Accompanying this series is a set of workbooks containing practice activities which are divided into chapters to match the teacher's resource book. Use a combination of the photocopiable pages in this book and the activities in the workbook to help children practise and consolidate spelling and vocabulary skills.

Differentiation

Activities in this book are not differentiated explicitly, although teacher notes may make suggestions for support or extension. Many of the activities can be used with the whole class with extra support provided through differentiated and open-ended questions, use of additional adults, mixed-ability paired or group work or additional input and consolidation before and/or after lessons. Some children may need support with the reading aspects of tasks in order to participate in the spelling objectives.

Using the CD-ROM

Below are brief guidance notes for using the CD-ROM. For more detailed information, see 'How to use this digital content' on the Main menu.

The CD-ROM follows the structure of the book and contains:
- All of the photocopiable pages.
- All of the poster pages in full colour.
- Answers provided, where relevant.
- Interactive on-screen activities linked to the photocopiable pages.

Getting started

Put the CD-ROM into your CD-ROM drive.
- For Windows users, the install wizard should autorun, if it fails to do so then navigate to your CD-ROM drive. Then follow the installation process.
- For Mac users, copy the disk image file to your hard drive. After it has finished copying double click it to mount the disk image. Navigate to the mounted disk image and run the installer. After installation the disk image can be unmounted and the DMG can be deleted from the hard drive.
- To install on a network, please see the ReadMe file located on the CD-ROM (navigate to your drive).

To complete the installation of the program you need to open the program and click 'Update' in the pop-up. Please note – this CD-ROM is web-enabled and the content will be downloaded from the internet to your hard-drive to populate the CD-ROM with the relevant resources. This only needs to be done on first use, after this you will be able to use the CD-ROM without an internet connection. If at any point any content is updated you will receive another pop-up upon start up with an internet connection.

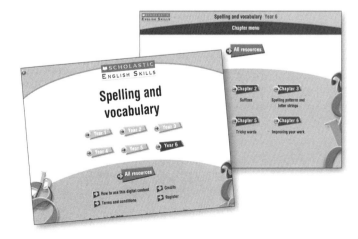

Main menu

The main menu is the first screen that appears. Here you can access: terms and conditions, registration links, how to use the digital content and credits. To access a specific year group click on the relevant button (NB only titles installed will be available). To browse all installed content click **All resources**.

Chapter menu

The Chapter menu provides links to all of the chapters or all of the resources for a specific year group. Clicking on the relevant Chapter icon will take you to the section screen where you can access the posters and the chapter's sections. Clicking on **All resources** will take you to a list of all the resources, where you can search by keyword or chapter for a specific resource.

Section menu

Here you can choose the relevant section to take you to its activity screen. You can also access the posters here.

Activity menu

Upon choosing a section from the section menu, you are taken to a list of resources for that section. Here you can access all of the photocopiable pages related to that section as well as the linked interactive activities.

All resources

All of the resources for a year group (if accessed via a Chapter menu) or all of the installed resources (if accessed via the Main menu). You can:

- Select a chapter and/or section by selecting the appropriate title from the drop-down menus.
- Search for key words by typing them into the search box.
- Scroll up or down the list of resources to locate the required resource.
- To launch a resource, simply click on the **Go** button.

Navigation

The resources (poster pages, photocopiable pages and interactive activities) all open in separate windows on top of the menu screen. To close a resource, click on the **x** in the top right-hand corner of the screen and this will return you to the menu screen.

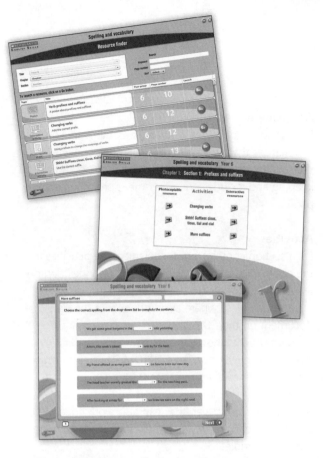

Closing a resource will not close the program. However, if you are in a menu screen, then clicking on the **x** will close the program. To return to a previous menu screen, you need to click on the **Back** button.

Teacher settings

In the top left-hand corner of the Main menu screen is a small **T** icon. This is the teacher settings area. It is password protected, the password is: login. This area will allow you to choose the print quality settings for interactive activities 'Default' or 'Best'. It will also allow you to check for updates to the program or re-download all content to the disk via **Refresh all content**.

Answers

The answers to the photocopiable pages can be found on the CD-ROM in the All resources menu. The answers are supplied in one document in a table-format, referencing the page number, title and answer for each relevant page. The pages that have answers are referenced in the 'Digital content' boxes on the teachers' notes pages. Unfortunately, due to the nature of English, not all pages can have answers provided because some activities require the children's own imaginative input or consist of a wider writing task.

Objectives

Objectives

Page	Section	English skills objective	To use knowledge of morphology and etymology in spelling.	To use further prefixes and suffixes and understand the guidelines for using them.	To continue to distinguish between homophones and other words which are often confused.	To understand that the spelling of some words needs to be learned specifically.	To use a dictionary to check the spelling and meaning of words.	To know how words are related by meaning as synonyms and antonyms. (Grammar appendix)	To use a thesaurus.	To understand the difference between vocabulary typical of informal speech and vocabulary appropriate for formal speech and writing. (Grammar appendix)	To proofread for spelling errors.
63	Word structure	To spell words with inflectional endings and understand the origin of words.	✓								
67	Borrowed words	To choose and use words by understanding their origin, meaning and usage.	✓								
71	Greek and Latin prefixes and suffixes	To investigate the use and spelling of prefixes and suffixes with Greek and Latin origin.	✓	✓							
79	Homophones and easily confused words	To spell homophones and other words that are easily confused.			✓						
83	Spelling tricky words	To understand that the spelling of some words needs to be learned specifically.				✓					
87	Strategies for spelling	To use a range of strategies as aids to spelling longer or tricky words.				✓					
95	Dictionary skills	To use a dictionary to check the spelling and meaning of words.					✓				
99	Synonyms and antonyms	To find and use synonyms and antonyms to extend vocabulary and improve writing.						✓			
103	Using a thesaurus	To use a thesaurus to find appropriate synonyms and antonyms.							✓		
107	Formal and informal vocabulary	To understand the difference between vocabulary typical of informal speech as well as formal speech and writing.								✓	
111	Checking and improving writing	To proofread for spelling errors and propose changes to vocabulary.									✓
115	Bringing it all together	To consolidate learning.	✓	✓				✓			✓

Chapter 4 — pages 63, 67, 71
Chapter 5 — pages 79, 83, 87
Chapter 6 — pages 95, 99, 103, 107, 111, 115

Chapter 1

Revisit and reinforce

Introduction

This chapter provides the children with the opportunity to revise elements of the curriculum covered in Year 5. They will revise the rules for adding prefixes and suffixes to root words, and gain confidence in using spelling patterns. Spelling is not something that can simply be absorbed, so providing the children with visual and auditory tools and practice is essential. Spelling a word is not just about the letters and sounds in a word but how the word is put together, hence understanding root words is a fundamental element of successful spelling. The children will also revise word families. For further practice, please see the 'Revisit and reinforce' section in the Year 6 workbook.

In this chapter

Poster notes

Suffixes and verb prefixes (page 10)

This poster summarises the revision elements of the chapter. Use the poster to focus on prefixes and suffixes the children have learned, reminding them that a root word is the core word but its spelling and function can change as other parts are added. Ask the children if they remember the meaning of any of the prefixes, and what effect they have – for instance, 'un' changes a word from positive (*happy*) to negative (*unhappy*). Look at the suffixes listed and discuss the effect that they have on the root word. Some suffixes change the word class – for example, verbs into nouns and adjectives: *confide* (verb)/*confidence* (noun)/*confident* (adjective); and nouns and adjectives into verbs: *soft* (adjective)/*soften* (verb); *intensity* (noun)/*intensify* (verb).

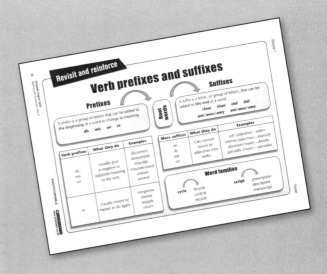

Revisit and reinforce

Verb prefixes and suffixes

Prefixes

A prefix is a group of letters that can be added to the beginning of a word to change its meaning.

dis   mis   un   re

Root words

Suffixes

A suffix is a letter, or group of letters, that can be added to the end of a word.

cious   tious   cial   tial

ant/ance/ancy   ent/ence/ency

Verb prefixes	What they do	Examples
dis mis un	Usually give a negative or opposite meaning to the verb.	disconnect disassemble misjudge misunderstand unload unravel
re	Usually means to repeat or do again.	reorganise rewrite reapply return

More suffixes	What they do	Examples
en ify ate ise	Can convert nouns or adjectives into verbs.	soft (adjective) – soften intense (adjective) – intensify donation (noun) – donate speciality (noun) – specialise

Word families

cycle   bicycle
cyclical
recycle

script   prescription
descriptive
manuscript

PHOTOCOPIABLE

Prefixes and suffixes

To practise using verb prefixes and choose suffixes correctly.

Background knowledge

In Year 5, the children learned some rules about adding prefixes to verbs and suffixes to root words and how these change the root or make new words. The children will recap some of these rules and practise adding prefixes and suffixes to root words, which may or may not change. The children should be aware of the number of syllables in a word and if the word begins or ends with a vowel or a consonant, as these may affect the spelling of a word. The prefixes 'un', 'dis' and 'mis' usually give a negative meaning. The suffixes 'cious', 'tious', 'cial' and 'tial' turn nouns into adjectives; if the root word ends in 'ce', 'cious' is used, and if 'tion', 'tious' is used. After a vowel, 'cial' is mainly used and 'tial' after a consonant. Turn verbs into nouns using 'ant', 'ance', 'ancy', 'ent', 'ence' and 'ency'; 'ent' and 'ant' can also make adjectives.

The purpose of the following photocopiable sheets is to revise and practise some of the verb prefixes and suffixes covered in the Year 5 book.

Activities

● **Photocopiable page 12 'Changing verbs'**
With a partner, challenge children to think of as many verbs as they can. Then see how many they can change to mean something different by adding the prefixes 'mis', 'dis' or 'un'. How has the meaning of the verbs been changed? Point out that these prefixes usually give a negative meaning. Discuss the prefix 're' and how it changes the meaning of a verb – it usually means 'to do again'. Encourage the use of a dictionary to check their verbs, reminding them that not all verbs can be given an opposite meaning – for example, there is no such verb as *untalk*.

● **Photocopiable page 13 'Shhh! Suffixes cious, tious, tial and cial'**
Children will learn how to turn nouns into adjectives by adding the suffix 'cious' or 'tious'. They will then unscramble anagrams to find words that end in 'cial' or 'tial'. Finally, they will complete sentences containing words they have made from the different suffixes.

● **Photocopiable page 14 'More suffixes'**
Discuss the rules of using the suffixes 'ence', 'ent', 'ency' and 'ance', 'ant', 'ancy' to make nouns. Use 'ance' if a related word has an /ai/ sound in the right position: *observation/observance*. Use 'ence' if a related word has an /e/ sound in the right position: *confident/confidence*. If the noun is made from a verb ending in 'y', 'ear' or 'ure', the suffix will be 'ance': *disappear/disappearance*. If a verb ends in 'ere' or 'er', the suffix will be 'ence': *prefer/preference*. Use 'ant' after an /ai/ sound in the right position: *hesitate/hesitant*, and 'ent' after an /e/ sound in the right position: *descend/descent*. After a hard 'c', use 'ancy': *vacant/vacancy*; and after a soft 'c' /see/ sound or 'g' /j/ sound, use 'ency': *agent/agency*.

Further ideas

● **Shared and independent reading:** As children read their own or guided reading books, invite them to add sticky notes to the working wall with examples of words beginning and ending in the prefixes and suffixes covered in this section.
● **Suffix to root word:** Set up an interactive whiteboard with activities that involve matching the correct suffix to a root word.
● **Quick-fire activities:** Call out verbs for the children to respond to with an appropriate prefix.

Digital content

On the digital component you will find:
● Printable versions of all three photocopiable pages.
● Answers to all three photocopiable pages.
● Interactive versions of all three photocopiable pages.

Name:

Changing verbs

■ Add the prefixes **mis**, **dis** or **un** to change the meaning of the following verbs.

lead	
load	
represent	
understand	
connect	
fasten	
cover	
tie	
spell	

■ Write the verbs to which these definitions apply. They all begin with the prefix **re**.

To start again _____

To remember something _____

To use waste again _____

To go back again _____

Prefixes and suffixes

Shhh! Suffixes cious, tious, tial and cial

■ Turn these nouns into adjectives by adding either the suffix **cious** or the suffix **tious**.

vice	
grace	
nutrition	
ferocity	
malice	
infection	

■ The words below are jumbled up. Unscramble the anagrams to find words that end in **cial** or **tial**.

alsoic   _____

canfeelibi   _____

liatini   _____

■ Add the **cious** or **tious** suffix to the words in the box below. use the words you have made to complete the following sentences.

tenacity	fiction	space	suspicion

The story about me winning the lottery was _____.

I saw a very _____ looking man in the bank.

Our new house has four bedrooms and is very _____.

The _____ explorer refused to give up.

SCHOLASTIC
www.scholastic.co.uk   **PHOTOCOPIABLE**   **Scholastic English Skills**
Spelling and vocabulary: Year 6   **13**

Name:

More suffixes

■ Add the suffix **ence** or **ance** to the following verbs to make nouns that you cannot see or touch.

dominate   _____

confident   _____

obey   _____

tolerate   _____

defend   _____

■ Choose the correct suffix for the words in brackets so that the following sentences make sense.

We got some great bargains in the (clear) _____ sale yesterday.

Amira, this week's talent (contest) _____, was by far the best.

He offered us some (guide) _____ on how to train our new dog.

The head teacher greeted the (apply) _____ for the teaching post.

After looking at a map for (reassure) _____, we knew we were on the right road.

■ Add the correct suffix to each of these words. Then write them in the appropriate column.

agent   pregnant   efficient   truant

ency	ancy

PHOTOCOPIABLE   ■SCHOLASTIC
www.scholastic.co.uk

Changing class

To convert nouns or adjectives into verbs using suffixes.

Background knowledge

In this section, the children will recap Year 5 work on converting nouns or adjectives into verbs using suffixes. The suffix 'en' can be added to adjectives to create verbs. If a word already ends in 'e', just add 'n' – for example, *ripe/ripen*. If a word ends in two consonants or a long vowel phoneme and a consonant, add 'en' – for example, *soft/soften*. If a word ends in a short vowel phoneme and a consonant, **double the consonant** and add 'en' – for example, *flat/flatten*. The suffixes 'ify', 'ise' and 'ate' can be used to convert nouns and adjectives into verbs: *intense* (adjective)/*intensify; donation* (noun)/*donate; speciality* (noun)/*specialise*.

The purpose of the following photocopiable sheets is to revise and practise adding suffixes to nouns and adjectives to change the word class, as covered in the Year 5 book.

Activities

● **Photocopiable page 16 'Transforming adjectives with the suffix en'**
Introduce each of the three rules above for adding the suffix 'en' to an adjective to create a verb – for example, *wide/widen, soft/soften* and *fat/fatten*. Collect adjectives from the class (ensure that you have examples of your own that can be converted into verbs). Explain that not all adjectives can have the suffix 'en' added to them, such as *beautiful*. Children will use their knowledge of the spelling rules to add 'en' to the adjectives in the activities and then write their own version of the spelling rules.

● **Photocopiable page 17 'When to use ise, ify or ate'**
Introduce the suffixes 'ise', 'ify' and 'ate', which can be added to the root words of nouns and adjectives to

make verbs – for example, *apology/apologise, horror/horrify* and *hesitation/hesitate*. Encourage the use of dictionaries to check spellings. Ask the children to recognise, between two different options, the correct spelling for various verbs in a passage. Then ask the children to reverse those verbs back to nouns.

● **Photocopiable page 18 'Which one?'**
Recap using all four suffixes. Before the children convert the noun or adjective into its verb form, they need to classify the words in the list as nouns or adjectives. A quick activity on whiteboards will help clarify that the children are secure in both; split the board into two columns, one nouns and the other adjectives, and the teacher then quick-fires a mixture of both.

Further ideas

● **Spelling mobiles:** Set up suffix mobiles from the ceiling. The children can add words ending in 'ise', 'ify', 'ate' and 'en' as they come across them in independent or shared reading activities.

● **Turn and match:** Give the children cards with a range of root words, both adjectives and nouns (such as *soft, intense, donation*), and the range of suffixes covered in the activities. Turn them face down on the table and then the children take turns to turn over two at a time, with the aim of matching a word with a suffix. If no suitable pair is turned over, the cards must be placed face down in the same position.

● **Root word suffix activity:** Display six words with an obvious root, such as *solid, fossil* and *broad*. Against a clock/timer tool, children individually or in pairs must turn the words into verbs on whiteboards.

Digital content

On the digital component you will find:
● Printable versions of all three photocopiable pages.
● Answers to all three photocopiable pages.
● Interactive version of 'When to use ise, ify or ate'.

Changing class

Transforming adjectives with the suffix en

■ Create a verb from each of the adjectives in bold to complete the sentences below. Then write three spelling rules for adding **en** to a word.

I like my jumpers **soft**, so my mum adds conditioner to the washing machine to

_____ them.

My big sister's **dark** hair had lightened in the sun so she bought a product that

would _____ it again.

My dog's collar was already **loose** but Dad decided to _____ it even more.

We used a rolling pin to roll the dough **flat** but Mum helped us _____ it properly.

The strawberries were **ripe** but Gran said to wait for them to _____ further before we picked them.

I dug a **deep** hole for the post to go in but my brother said I should

_____ it further to ensure the post didn't fall over.

Spelling rule 1: _____

Spelling rule 2: _____

Spelling rule 3: _____

■ Change these adjectives into verbs. Then put them all into a short passage.

sad	bright	length	fright	thick

_____

_____

_____

_____

Changing class

When to use ise, ify or ate

■ Turn the following nouns into verbs by using the suffixes **ise**, **ify** or **ate**.

apology	
magnification	
indication	
hesitation	
priority	
modification	
horror	
classification	
advertisement	

■ Circle the correctly spelled word in the brackets in this passage.

We tried to (**pacify**/**peacify**) our distraught neighbour who thought his money had been stolen. My mother (**sympathised**/**sympafied**) with the old man as she has been robbed herself. The true nature of what had actually happened to the money was soon (**clarificated**/**clarified**) – he remembered that he had spent it to (**advertise**/**advertify**) for a cleaner. He (**apologied**/**apologised**) to everyone and said that he was getting forgetful. My mother gently (**indicted**/**indicated**) that he already had a cleaner; she had just arrived at his house.

■ Now turn the correctly spelled verbs in the brackets above into nouns. The first has been done for you.

pacify → peace

Name:

Changing class

Which one?

■ Put the following words into the correct adjective or noun column in the tables below. Then turn them into verbs using either **en, ate, ify** or **ise**. Watch out though – one word in the list is both an adjective AND a noun.

hard	note
pollen	mesmerising
deep	improvisation
pure	horrible
classification	hyphen
apology	material
medicine	clarification
tight	short
fossil	terrible
solid	broad
clear	

Adjective	Verb	Noun	Verb

Word families

Objective

To understand how words are related in form and meaning and use this knowledge to aid spelling.

Background knowledge

Knowledge of word families can help children to remember silent letters when they are sounded in certain word families – for example, *sign/signature* and *bomb/bombastic*, and when vowels are unstressed/stressed – for example, *finite/definite/definition*. Thinking of and collecting words with the same root and grouping them into word families can help children to work out the meanings of the root words for themselves.

The purpose of the following photocopiable sheets is to revisit word families, as covered in the Year 5 book.

Activities

● **Photocopiable page 20 'Make a word family'**
Challenge children to find as many derivatives as they can for each of the root words provided. They could cut the root words out, glue them into their book and write the derivatives around each one. Who can create the largest word family? Observe whether individuals notice that some words in certain word families sound out letters that are silent in other derivations – for example, the 'g' in *sign* is sounded out in *signatory* and the 'n' in autumn is sounded out in *autumnal*. Similarly, some vowel sounds become unstressed – for example, *finite, definite, definition* and *medicine, medicinal*.

● **Photocopiable page 21 'Take me home'**
In this sorting activity, children can write the word families in one of four houses outlined on the paper as they identify them. Discuss the etymology – the study of the origin of words and the way in which their meanings have changed throughout history. 'Trans' comes from the Latin, meaning 'across': does this knowledge now help them know the meanings of the words they have grouped? 'Auto' comes from the Greek, meaning 'self'

or 'one's own': does knowing this help them with the meaning of the words they have grouped? And, similarly, 'tract' and 'rupt' both come from Latin: 'tract' comes from the verb *trahere*, meaning 'to pull', and in late Middle English it meant duration of time; 'rupt' comes from *eruptus*, meaning 'burst forth/broken'. Does this knowledge help with the meaning of their words – for example, a volcano erupting?

● **Photocopiable page 22 'Happy families'**
In this activity, children will continue to find derivatives for the words provided, thus creating word families. It can be extended for more confident learners by encouraging them to go beyond just two words.

Further ideas

● **Card game:** Place some cards with root words written on them in the middle of each table in the classroom. Using a dictionary to help them, children take it in turns (in pairs) to turn over a card and then write down as many derivatives as they can. They hide their findings and then swap the card with another two on their table. Compare findings once all the cards have been looked at.

● **Odd one out:** Create some word families but include some nonsense, invented words. The children need to find the odd one out. Alternatively, the children can create the word families and the odd one out and swap with another partnership/table group.

● **Creating sentences:** Challenge the children to write a sentence containing *all* the words they can think of from one word family.

Digital content

On the digital component you will find:
● Printable versions of all three photocopiable pages.
● Answers to all three photocopiable pages.
● Interactive version of 'Take me home'.

Name:

Word families

Make a word family

■ Cut each word out and see how many words you can write around it that belong in the same word family.

profession	sign
phone	use
species	finite
company	rotate
circus	cycle
port	medicine

PHOTOCOPIABLE

Word families

Take me home

■ All these words have become separated from their word families. Help to reunite them by identifying their common root and putting them in a house with the rest of their family.

disruption

tractor   subtract   interrupt

autopilot

autopsy   traction

attract   abrupt   autocratic

autobiographical   transferal   translate

attracted

corrupt   retract   transatlantic   transfer

transmit

interruption   transformer

transformation

autobiography

attractive   transport

bankrupt   intransitive

distract   ruptured

automatic

eruption   attraction

autoimmune

corrupted   autograph   automation

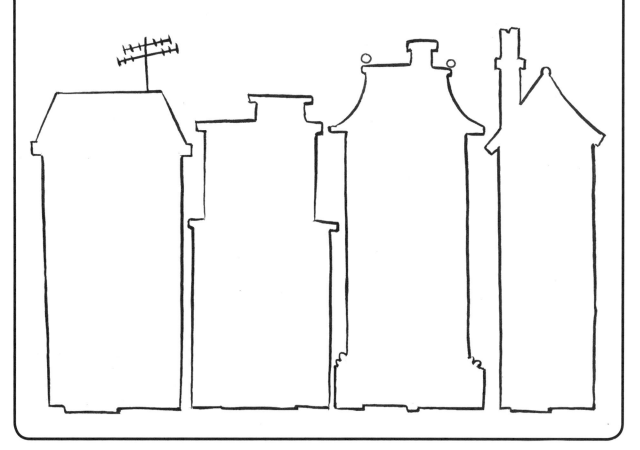

Name:

Word families

Happy families

■ Find two more words to make a word family in each case.

finish   _____   _____

memory   _____   _____

care   _____   _____

picture   _____   _____

build   _____   _____

help   _____   _____

dine   _____   _____

telephone   _____   _____

bicycle   _____   _____

supermarket   _____   _____

autograph   _____   _____

define   _____   _____

table   _____   _____

Assessment

Assessment grid

The following grid shows the main objectives and activities covered in this chapter. You can use the grid to locate activities that cover a particular focus that you are keen to monitor.

Objective	Page	Activity title
To use further prefixes and suffixes and understand the guidelines for adding them.	12	Changing verbs
	13	Shhh! Suffixes cious, tious, tial and cial
	14	More suffixes
	16	Transforming adjectives with the suffix en
	17	When to use ise, ify or ate
	18	Which one?
To use and spell endings 'cial' and 'tial' and 'cious' and 'tious'.	13	Shhh! Suffixes cious, tious, tial and cial
To use and spell words ending in 'ant', 'ance', 'ent', 'ence' and 'ency'.	14	More suffixes
To revise word family work to aid spelling.	20	Make a word family
	21	Take me home
	22	Happy families

Observation and record keeping

As the children work through the photocopiable sheets in this chapter, highlight any misconceptions about the prefixes or suffixes that they choose. Make notes of individual targets against a class list. Encourage children to keep a word bank to record challenging or interesting words and to share these with a partner. Encourage them too, to ensure their word bank is accessible during all writing tasks.

In the assessment activity, children will choose the appropriate prefix or suffix for the words provided.

Assessment activity

● **What you need**
Photocopiable page 24 'Prefixes, suffixes and word families'.
● **What to do**
Remind children that verb meanings can be changed by adding prefixes. Often the meaning is opposite or negative – for example, by using the prefixes 'un', 'dis' or 'mis'. The prefix 're' means to do again or repeat – for example, *address/readdress* (to address something again). Remind the children that the spelling of the root word may change quite dramatically when adding a suffix – for example, *clear/clarity* and *peace/pacify*. The assessment page consists of three tasks to cover prefixes, suffixes and word families.

Differentiation

● Support less confident learners, ensuring both their understanding of terminology (prefix, suffix, root word) as well as spelling skills.
● More confident learners will use terminology confidently in discussion. Encourage them to identify word families as they read and write.

Further learning

● **Etymology:** Use words found in other subjects as the basis for further research into etymology, especially those with prefixes – for example, 'dec' means 'one tenth', so what does *decimate* mean?
● **Dictionary:** Encourage the children to use dictionaries fully, especially to check the spelling of suffixed and prefixed words.
● **Quick-fire activities:** Say a word out loud that needs a prefix to make it opposite or negative in meaning, then ask the children to call out the new word as an instant response. Have fun with the prefix 're' by using it to make nonsensical verbs such as *resleep* or *retalk*. Use this same format to do a similar activity for suffixes, but display the root words first. Progress from verbal responses to writing on whiteboards to verify that spelling rules have been taken into account.

Name:

Assessment

Prefixes, suffixes and word families

■ Add an appropriate prefix to the following verbs to change their meaning. Some words have more than one possibility.

wind		trace	
think		like	
cover		heat	
believe		stitch	
represent		consider	

■ Choose an appropriate suffix to change these nouns and adjectives into verbs.

Nouns

identity   _____

standard   _____

drama   _____

abbreviation   _____

Adjectives

weak   _____

pure   _____

dead   _____

clear   _____

■ Find two more words that belong to each of the following words to make a word family.

Word families

create   _____   _____

house   _____   _____

family   _____   _____

except   _____   _____

Chapter 2

Suffixes

Introduction

This chapter looks at suffixes. Children often rely heavily on a spellchecker when using a computer to write. When they realise that the checker only picks up errors in spelling patterns and not errors in meaning and usage, they become aware of the need to edit their work themselves. Knowledge of the spelling rules for adding suffixes is fundamental to good spelling, and in the activities in this section the children are given plenty of opportunities to practise their skills. For further practice, please see the 'Suffixes' section in the Year 6 workbook.

Poster notes

Suffixes and hyphens (page 26)

The poster provides a generic definition of the term *suffix* and can be used to introduce the concepts as a reference point and also for support during independent work. Look at each of the suffixes introduced on the poster and invite the children to suggest words that contain each one. Can they identify nouns, verbs, adjectives and adverbs?

The second example on the poster shows how hyphens can be used to avoid ambiguity. Ask the children for sentences containing the examples shown, to establish that they understand the differences in meaning.

In this chapter

Which ending? page 27	To spell words ending in the suffixes 'able' or 'ible', and 'ably' or 'ibly'.
Adding suffixes page 31	To add suffixes beginning with vowel letters to words ending in 'fer'.
Transforming words using suffixes page 35	To extend understanding of the use of suffixes to change the class of a word.
Using hyphens page 39	To use hyphens in spelling to avoid ambiguity.
Assessment page 43	Activities and ideas to assess use of suffixes.

SUFFIXES AND HYPHENS

Suffixes

A suffix is a letter or group of letters that can be added to **the end** of a word. Sometimes a suffix will change the word class – for example, verbs to adjectives and verbs to adverbs:

manage ↪ manageable

believe ↪ believable

notice ↪ noticeably

eat ↪ edible

horrify ↪ horribly

sense ↪ sensibly

They can also change verbs to nouns and nouns to verbs:

realise ↪ realisation

imagination ↪ imagine

photography ↪ photograph

And they can change the verb tense:

change – changed

kick – kicked

finish – finished

rely – relied

reply – replied

cry – cried

HYPHENS

Hyphens can be used to avoid ambiguity. Look at the differences in meaning between these pairs of words:

recover/re-cover

represent/re-present

and between these phrases:

a man-eating shark

a man eating shark

my quick-thinking teacher

my quick thinking teacher

Which ending?

Objective

To spell words ending in the suffixes 'able' or 'ible', and 'ably' or 'ibly'.

Background knowledge

In these activities the children will learn some strategies for making choices between suffixes when spelling words. Explain to the children that the suffixes 'ible', 'ibly', 'able' and 'ably' can be added to verbs to change them into adjectives and adverbs – for example, *notice/noticeable/noticeably* and *terrify/terrible/terribly*. In general, the choice of suffix 'ible' or 'ibly' and 'able' or 'ably' relies on whether the word that is left when dropping the suffix is a whole root word – for example, *agree + able/ably*. There is no fixed rule for which spelling to use. Most words ending with 'e' drop the 'e' when adding 'able'; most words with a soft g (/j/ sound) or /s/ sound use 'ible'; most words with a hard c or g sound use 'able' and words ending in 'ce' or 'ge' keep their 'e' before 'able', to keep the sound soft.

Activities

● **Photocopiable page 28 'When to use ible or able'**
Ask the children to read the words in the first section of the photocopiable sheet – what do they notice about each one? Once the children have identified that they end in either the suffix 'able' or 'ible', choose some of the words for the children to put in a sentence and then ask them what word class each word is (such as adjective). Then ask them to work out the root word – for example, *reverse*. Explore words with no obvious root, such as *possible, susceptible* or *incredible*.

● **Photocopiable page 29 'Should I use ibly or ably?'**
Discuss the general rules for adding 'ible' or 'able' with the children and then ask them what they think the rules for adding 'ibly' and 'ably' might be. Discuss

any patterns that they notice when they change verbs into adjectives and whether they think these might be transferable to making adverbs. Recap what an adverb is if necessary.

● **Photocopiable page 30 'Spot the imposter'**
Probability is an important part of learning to spell, and children are given the opportunity to develop this systematically by grouping words according to their patterns. Children love games where they are asked to spot the odd one out, or find the incorrect spelling; some will need dictionaries to help them, whereas for others it will be simply recognition of the correct spelling.

Further ideas

● **Spelling challenges:** Set a *Who Wants to be a Millionaire*-style quiz for all the suffixes used in the chapter, with multiple-choice answers.
● **Spot the suffix:** Encourage children to write words ending in 'able', 'ible', 'ably' and 'ibly' on sticky notes and add them to a large poster on a working wall. Divide the poster into two columns, adjectives in one and adverbs in the other, to consolidate their understanding of these word classes. Do something similar for the 'fer' suffix, but divide the poster into stressed and unstressed columns.

Digital content

On the digital component you will find:
● Printable versions of all three photocopiable pages.
● Answers to all three photocopiable pages.
● Interactive versions of 'When to use ible or able' and 'Should I use ibly or ably?'.

Name:

Which ending?

When to use ible or able

■ Read these words and underline the suffixes (**ible** or **able**).

■ Some of the words are whole words when you take the suffix away. Write them in the root word box.

achievable

responsible

edible

breakable

respectable

enjoyable

reversible

available

possible

agreeable

susceptible

comfortable

incredible

visible

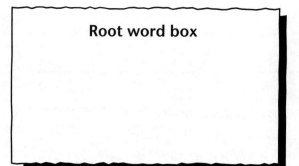

Root word box

■ Finish this sentence: All the words in this box take the suffix _____ .

■ Look at the root words listed below. Write out the new **ible** or **able** words in the appropriate columns.

horror	forgive
adore	notice
destruct	advise
misery	break
reverse	recognise
terror	comfort
identity	fashion

ible	able

Clue
If you can say '**I am able to…**' to the root word, then the suffix is most likely **able**.

Which ending?

Should I use ibly or ably?

■ Add either **ibly** or **ably** to turn these words into adverbs.

flex		depend		desire	
horror		sense		suit	
vision		consider		reason	
rely		understand		love	
response		irresistible		defence	

■ Now check them using your dictionary. Rewrite any that were incorrect and learn them using the Look, Say, Cover, Write, Check method.

■ Change these verbs into adverbs so that each sentence makes sense.

Forgive   There is a _____ excellent reason for Jon being late.

Regret   We were _____ unfit and therefore lost the match.

Rely   We were _____ informed that we had passed our tests.

Consider   My teacher was _____ later than expected due to traffic.

Notice   My dog's health has _____ improved in the past week.

Reason   My parents let me stay up _____ late on New Year's Eve.

Understand   Our guests were _____ tired after their long flight.

■ SCHOLASTIC
www.scholastic.co.uk   **PHOTOCOPIABLE**   Scholastic English Skills
Spelling and vocabulary: Year 6   **29**

Name:

Which ending?

Spot the imposter

■ Circle the incorrectly spelled word in the brackets in each of these sentences.

My homework this week was (**incredibly/incredably**) difficult.

The success of the magician's trick was to make the rabbit (**invisable/invisible**).

It was an (**understandably/understandibly**) busy week but we could relax at the weekend.

The boy's handwriting was so (**illegeble/illegible**) that his paper could not be marked.

Our head teacher announced that leaving litter on the playground was (**unacceptable/unacceptible**).

After our teacher told us off, there was barely an (**audible/audable**) sound in the room.

■ Now read the passage below and underline the adjectives and adverbs ending with the suffixes **able**, **ably**, **ible** and **ibly**. However, some of the words have been spelled incorrectly. Write the correct versions of these words in the box below.

Last week, our parents took us on a terribly long and boring trip to the countryside where the weather was quite changable: one minute it was blowing a gale, the next it was considerably calmer. At the end of an interminibly long walk, Dad said (quite audibly, considering the wind), "Look, Snowden is just visible from up here!" Really, it was virtually impossible to see anything in the dense mist. My sister and I were feeling quite miserible, not to mention chilly, and we probably seemed quite ungrateful to our parents. Luckily, after a totally inedable lunch, which Mum told the waiter was quite unacceptable, we got back in the car and headed home. We got back incredibly late due to the traffic and an irresponsable farmer who blocked the road with his sheep for a good two miles!

PHOTOCOPIABLE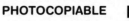
www.scholastic.co.uk

Adding suffixes

Objective

To add suffixes beginning with vowel letters to words ending in 'fer'.

Background knowledge

Children in Year 6 should know the difference between a stressed and an unstressed syllable. When adding a suffix beginning with a vowel letter to a word ending in 'fer', it is helpful for the children to say the word aloud to identify where the stress or emphasis falls so they can decide whether they need to double the 'r'. If the syllable 'fer' is still stressed after the suffix is added, the 'r' is doubled – for example, *referral*; if the syllable 'fer' is unstressed, the 'r' is not doubled – for example, *preference*.

Activities

● **Photocopiable page 32 'Stressed or unstressed?'**
The first part of the first activity is to ensure that children can identify stressed and unstressed syllables; it doesn't deal with the 'fer' rule: the doubling (or not) of the letter 'r'. The second part moves on to this once they are secure in knowing the difference between stressed and unstressed syllables. It is useful for the children to say the words out loud, initially with exaggerated emphasis, to help establish whether the syllable is stressed or unstressed.

● **Photocopiable page 33 'Single or double?'**
In this activity the children are seeing the words in context and are applying learned spelling rules. Children should be encouraged to use a dictionary to help them write the sentences using the words in context, as they just might need clarification on the meaning of some, but only after they first have a go at spelling the words correctly.

● **Photocopiable page 34 'Finding fer words'**
In this word search activity, children will hunt for hidden words containing the letter string 'fer', then decide – based on the spelling of either single 'r' or double 'r' – which ones stress the 'fer' syllable and which ones don't.

Further ideas

● **Card game:** In the middle of each table, space out some cards showing words such as *transfer* or *prefer* and suffixes starting with a vowel – for example, 'ence' or 'ed' – face down. Children have their own 'bank' of cards showing the letter 'r'. In pairs, children take it in turns to turn over two cards at a time. They won't always get a 'fer' and a suffix – the game is a bit like 'fish'; in other words, it is a memory game too. If they get two of the same kind, they replace them face down in the exact same spot. As and when they get a 'fer' word and a suffix, they need to decide whether they will need to use one of their 'r' cards, depending on the syllable stress.

● **Double or quit:** Create some incorrectly spelled words, where the 'r' is doubled incorrectly or not doubled incorrectly, and show them on the whiteboard. The winner is the first to write the correct spelling of all the words. Take this to the next level by including some correctly spelled words too.

Digital content

On the digital component you will find:
● Printable versions of all three photocopiable pages.
● Answers to all three photocopiable pages.

Name:

Adding suffixes

Stressed or unstressed?

■ Say the words below out loud. Then underline the syllable that is **stressed** in each.

dismay	thorough
observe	circle
dislike	runway
final	snowman
garden	tractor
candle	horrid

■ Now look at the words below, which end in the letter string **fer**. Remember the rule: *double the r if the fer syllable is stressed when you add a suffix starting with a vowel.*

■ Complete the table below, following the rule above (the shaded boxes are for words that cannot be completed).

	ed	al	ing	ence
refer				
infer				
transfer				
prefer				
confer				

PHOTOCOPIABLE

Adding suffixes

Single or double?

■ Complete the sentences below by adding an appropriate suffix to each root word, remembering the spelling rule.

The football (refer) _____ said the goal was off-side.

After the (confer) _____, our head teacher was very tired.

Our dog was (refer) _____ to a specialist vet.

My mum (offer) _____ to take us swimming.

We went to Spain last year but I much (prefer) _____ France.

■ Add a suffix to each of the following words to make a new word. Then write a sentence using each in context.

differ + _____ = _____

_____

offer + _____ = _____

_____

refer + _____ = _____

_____

confer + _____ = _____

_____

prefer + _____ = _____

_____

Name:

Adding suffixes

Finding fer words

■ Find the fourteen words containing the **fer** letter string hidden in this word search. Then place each word in the correct column in the table below.

c	d	p	i	n	f	e	r	r	e	d	g
o	e	d	r	f	j	a	k	i	i	n	i
n	r	p	i	e	c	g	q	f	i	n	n
f	e	h	i	f	f	s	f	r	f	b	f
e	f	c	o	n	f	e	r	e	n	c	e
r	f	t	v	a	r	e	r	e	m	s	r
r	o	e	k	e	f	r	r	e	e	x	e
i	r	f	n	s	i	e	u	i	n	r	n
n	p	c	n	n	o	f	b	y	n	c	c
g	e	a	g	j	i	e	l	a	u	g	e
m	r	e	c	n	e	r	e	f	e	r	b
t	c	o	n	f	e	r	r	e	d	f	j

fer stressed	**fer** unstressed

PHOTOCOPIABLE

SCHOLASTIC
www.scholastic.co.uk

Transforming words using suffixes

Objective

To extend understanding of the use of suffixes to change the class of a word.

Background knowledge

A root word is a word or part of a word to which prefixes and suffixes can be added to make new words from the same word family. The suffixes that are used in this chapter to change verbs to nouns are: 'tion', 'sion', 'ment', 'ance', 'age', 'al' and 'ture'. Exposure to the root verbs and their respective nouns will help children learn how the suffix addition affects the spelling of the root. For example, when adding the suffix 'ure' to *fail*, you just add it; however, the spelling of both *furnish* and *sign* needs to be changed. Some general rules that can help children are: verbs ending in 'ck' usually add the suffix 'age' (*block + age = blockage)*, and verbs ending in 'de' usually add the suffix 'sion' (*protrude + sion = protrusion*).

The most effective way to teach children these spelling patterns is by exposure and use.

Activities

● **Photocopiable page 36 'Verbs to nouns'**
The children are given a list of verbs and seven suffixes that are commonly used to transform verbs into nouns. As they write the nouns into the correct suffix box, encourage them to say the words out loud and think: *Does it sound right?* Further consolidation of the correct suffix use occurs when the children use a dictionary and investigate how to use the nouns in a sentence of their own on the back of the photocopiable sheet. Discuss how the root word changes in some instances – for example, *arrive* becomes *arrival,* yet in others this is not the case – such as *block* becoming *blockage*.
● **Photocopiable page 37 'Nouns to verbs'**
The children are given ten sentences that include a noun made by adding a suffix to a verb. As they investigate

the noun to establish the root word, they will be breaking up the word into root and suffix and this will reinforce the spelling patterns of adding suffixes. By writing new sentences using the root word as a verb, they will be consolidating their understanding.
● **Photocopiable page 38 'Revisiting suffixes'**
In this activity the children add suffixes to change adjectives to nouns, using 'ness', 'ity' and 'y'. Explain to the children that they need to think about how the spelling will change when adding the correct suffix to the adjective. Support less confident learners by using *brief* as an example and asking: 'Should we add the suffix 'ness' or 'ity', making *briefness* or *brevity*?' Encourage them to think about whether the root word needs to change, or just the final letter, when words end in 'y'. Allow children who need support to use a dictionary to help them when they cannot decide between the suffixes 'ness' or 'ity'.

Further ideas

● **Word cards:** Make cards of the suffixes and verbs found in the activities on the photocopiable sheets. Encourage the children to join the cards together to change the verb into a noun.
● **Guided reading:** As you read through the text with the children, see how many nouns they can spot that have come from adjectives, such as *difficulty* from *difficult.*
● **Silly sentences:** Have fun with nouns, verbs and adjectives by challenging the children to write sentences containing a word from the same family in adjective, noun and verb word class: *I imagine that the imaginative artist used his imagination.*

Digital content

On the digital component you will find:
● Printable versions of all three photocopiable pages.
● Answers to all three photocopiable pages.
● Interactive version of 'Verbs to nouns'.

Name:

Verbs to nouns

■ Change the verbs in the list into nouns by writing the noun into the correct suffix box.

tion	ment	ance

age	ure	sion

to appreciate	to depart	to maintain
to adjust	to endure	to modify
to arrange	to erode	to press
to arrive	to explode	to protrude
to block	to fail	to recognise
to break	to furnish	to sign
to conclude	to improve	to survive
to cultivate	to insure	to transform
to determine	to leak	to wreck

al

■ SCHOLASTIC
www.scholastic.co.uk

Nouns to verbs

■ Each of these sentences contains a noun that has been made by adding a suffix to a verb. Underline the root word (verb) in each of these nouns and write a sentence of your own using the verb instead of the noun. Use a dictionary to help you and check that you have used the words as verbs and not adjectives in your sentences. The first one has already been done as an example.

1. When the tree reaches <u>matur</u>ity it will be ten metres high.

   When I mature I might be 180cm tall. _____

2. Donald has a vivid imagination.

   _____

3. Can you find the solution to the problem before the lesson ends?

   _____

4. Make a shallow depression in the surface by lightly pushing with your thumb.

   _____

5. Information retrieval is an important skill.

   _____

6. Their laughter rang through the vast hall.

   _____

7. The variation in temperature in this greenhouse ranges from 0 degrees to 40 degrees.

   _____

8. When the pictures were printed, we all admired her photography.

   _____

9. To my amazement we won, despite having fewer players on our team.

   _____

10. To the best of my knowledge, he finished the game himself.

   _____

Name:

Revisiting suffixes

■ Add a suffix to change these adjectives to nouns (for example, *happy* becomes *happiness*).

Adjective	Noun
lazy	
clear	
bright	
choppy	
brief	
soft	
scarce	
able	
wary	
flexible	
damp	
difficult	
pretty	
tricky	

■ Think of a rule to help you spell nouns made from adjectives.

Using hyphens

Objective

To use hyphens in spelling to avoid ambiguity.

Background knowledge

Remind children what the word *ambiguity* means – where a word or sentence can have more than one meaning. In this section we are looking specifically at hyphens in spelling, where a hyphen may join a prefix to a root word and where a compound word is made using a hyphen. When the prefix ends in a vowel and the root word begins with a vowel (for example, *co-ordinate*), a hyphen is used to join the two, although also explain that very often *coordinate* is written *without* the hyphen. In other examples, the joining of a prefix to a root word with a hyphen differentiates the meaning of the same word *without* a hyphen, such as *recover* and *re-cover*, where *recover* means to return to normal or find something that was lost and *re-cover* means to cover something again. Compound words may be made using a hyphen to avoid ambiguity too – for example, *I saw a man eating shark* versus *I saw a man-eating shark*.

Activities

● **Photocopiable page 40 'Which word?'**
Before starting this activity, ask the children to think of words where the prefix is joined by a hyphen. They may come up with *co-operate* or *co-ordinate* but might need guidance when with words such as *recover* and *re-cover*. Discuss the difference in meaning of some examples before presenting them with other words and asking them to discuss with a partner the possible different meanings depending on whether or not the prefix is joined with a hyphen, such as *reform* and *re-form*.
● **Photocopiable page 41 'What do you mean?'**
Explain the meaning of the word *ambiguous* and see if the children can come up with any examples of a word or sentence that is ambiguous. Some children may talk about ambiguity in terms of missing

commas – for example, *Let's eat Granny* versus *Let's eat, Granny*. Explain that the hyphen also can bring a different meaning to written English – ask them what the difference is between a 'quick thinking teacher' and a 'quick-thinking teacher'; what is a 'thinking teacher'? Discuss the fact that in the sentences on the photocopiable sheet, regardless of missing hyphens, the punctuation is inaccurate – if the intention *was* that the writer liked 'sugar, free tea and coffee', then there should be a comma between 'sugar' and 'free'.
● **Photocopiable page 42 'Where's my hyphen?'**
Building on the previous activity, children need to sift through the text to find pairs of words (or more than two) that should be joined by a hyphen to make compound adjectives. Some, though not all, of the missing hyphens could lead to ambiguity, such as *quick thinking/quick-thinking*.

Further ideas

● **Guided and shared reading:** Discuss the use of hyphens as they appear, not only where they may be used to avoid ambiguity but also where compound words are made and to indicate a line break. Discuss misconceptions – for example, where children identify a dash or a pair of dashes as hyphens.
● **Silly sentences:** How many 'silly sentences' can the children create where the omission or inclusion of a hyphen results in ambiguous meaning? For example, *The man eating crocodile was re-covering*.
● **Pair-me-up:** Give children sets of cards with one half of a compound word written on each one, such as *quick* or *thinking*. The objective is to pair them up correctly, joining them with a hyphen from the 'hyphen card bank'. This game could include words with hyphenated prefixes for more confident learners.

Digital content

On the digital component you will find:
● Printable versions of all three photocopiable pages.
● Answers to 'What do you mean?' and 'Where's my hyphen?'.
● Interactive version of 'What do you mean?'.

Name:

Using hyphens

Which word?

The following pairs of words have different meanings – the only difference is that one has a hyphen to join the prefix to the root word and one does not.

■ Read the words aloud. Then write a sentence for each to show the difference in meaning. The first one has been done for you.

resign: *My mum decided to* **resign** *from her job after she had my baby brother.*

re-sign: *Our head teacher had to* **re-sign** *all the reports after spilling coffee over them.*

recover: _____

_____

re-cover: _____

_____

resent: _____

_____

re-sent: _____

_____

repress: _____

_____

re-press: _____

_____

Using hyphens

What do you mean?

The following sentences are ambiguous – they could have more than one meaning. To make sense as they are, some would need a comma but even then, they'd still sound a bit odd. What do you make of a 'thick, skinned and patient' rabbit, for example?

■ Find the guilty pairs of words that should have been written as hyphenated compound words and rewrite the sentence correctly on the line below.

When I was in Australia, I saw a man eating shark.

_____

I like sugar free tea and coffee.

_____

Most of the time travellers like to use spaceships.

_____

He was a hard working employee of the restaurant owner.

_____

My mum likes reading magazine style books.

_____

In our new house we have a stainless steel kitchen.

_____

The good looking contestant's high pitched singing was very enjoyable.

_____

My thick skinned rabbit wasn't affected by my brother's teasing.

_____

Name:

Using hyphens

Where's my hyphen?

■ Read this passage. Then decide which words should be joined with a hyphen. Write the words in the box below.

My sister is a quick thinking girl who works full time in the local leisure centre. She used to be a part time, self employed gardener but she came face to face with too many ultra demanding customers who wanted things such as custom built sheds and state of the art patios. One particular incident left her wide eyed and open mouthed: a bad tempered, grey haired old lady blamed her for the lack of blooms in her border flowers! My sister, normally a kind, good hearted girl, sarcastically replied that she had no control over the weather and perhaps the woman should employ a magician to do her garden.

She is much happier in her new role, especially as she is sport mad and has come into contact with the England team goalkeeper on a few occasions. From what I've heard, she's the manager's blue eyed girl and destined to go far.

Assessment

Assessment grid

The following grid shows the main objectives and activities covered in this chapter. You can use the grid to locate activities that cover a particular focus that you are keen to monitor.

Objective	Page	Activity title
To spell words ending in the suffixes 'able' or 'ible', and 'ably' or 'ibly'.	28	When to use ible or able
	29	Should I use ibly or ably?
	30	Spot the imposter
To add suffixes beginning with vowel letters to words ending in 'fer'.	32	Stressed or unstressed?
	33	Single or double?
	34	Finding fer words
To convert nouns or adjectives into verbs using suffixes.	36	Verbs to nouns
	37	Nouns to verbs
	38	Revisiting suffixes
To use hyphens to avoid ambiguity.	40	Which word?
	41	What do you mean?
	42	Where's my hyphen?

Observation and record keeping

In this dictation assessment activity, children will 'listen well' and 'spell well' words in context that end in the suffixes covered in this chapter. The third dictation passage deals with hyphenated compound words and prefixes joined to a root word with a hyphen. Using a class list, record areas of difficulty in the children's spelling and use this to inform future spelling homework. Stressing the syllable 'fer' in words such as *referral* will help children remember the spelling rule. Hyphens are more challenging, especially where there are inconsistencies between UK English and US English, but these can lead to interesting class discussions.

Assessment activity

● **What you need**

Photocopiable page 44 'Listen well, spell well', writing materials.

● **What to do**

Remind children about the different suffixes they have covered in this chapter and how hyphens can form compound words, usually adjectives, as well as join prefixes to root words. Remember that omitting the hyphen can lead to *ambiguity*. When reading the dictation passages, emphasise the words in bold, telling children in advance that these emphasised words are related to their learning in this chapter and that the spelling focus is on them.

Differentiation

● Support less confident learners with dictations 2 and 3 by working in a small group and emphasising the words in bold as you read. It would be useful to read the dictations out first so they can hear the words in context before starting to write the passages down. For these children, spread the dictations over two to three days if necessary.

● With more confident learners, do not emphasise the words in bold in the dictations.

Further learning

● **Dictionary work:** With one dictionary per child, or one per two children, discuss how stressed syllables are indicated (usually by an apostrophe before or after the stressed syllable – this should be made clear at the start of the dictionary). Look up words such as *refer* and *inference* and note the difference in where the stress indicator is, relating it to the spelling rule.

Name:

Assessment

Listen well, spell well

Dictation 1

The clown's performance was **laughably** poor. After an **acceptable** start, his performance went **rapidly** downhill. After his **failure** to make anyone laugh, especially after his **incredibly** weak **explosion** from a canon, we all agreed that we **preferred** the two trapeze artists, who had **transferred** from the famous Moscow Circus Troup.

Dictation 2

When we went on safari, the water from the river was quite **drinkable**. Our meals, however, were often **inedible**, but we **inferred** from the cook that nothing else was available. I must say, my **preference** would be to eat in the local restaurant – a **referral** from our neighbours, who were there last year. For such an **incredibly** expensive trip, you'd think all standards would be high!

Dictation 3

We decided that, as a **short-term** issue, being so far from our new school would not be inconvenient. However, the **long term** after Easter was going to cause some problems. Dad said he would have to **re-examine** the travel options but it would have to wait as he was **recovering** from a bad cold. My **quick-thinking** sister suggested we take the **ultra-fast** tram service from the suburbs into the city centre, from where it was a short bus ride to school. We just needed to study the timetables. Mum produced an old, **dog-eared** timetable that would be fine if we **re-covered** it.

Chapter 3

Spelling patterns and letter strings

Introduction

Learning spelling rules is great until the exceptions get in the way. The rule *i before e except after c* is one of the most widely used rules. However, there are a number of exceptions that simply need to be learned, where the pronunciation of 'ei' or 'ie' is not /ee/. Similarly, the letter string 'ough' has many different pronunciations; encourage the children to read aloud the words on the poster and discuss the different sounds. Looking at the etymology of words with children when discussing silent letters is useful; for example, they might be surprised to know that *knight* was once pronounced with a hard /k/ sound at the beginning, *k-night,* and that the 'gh' also used to represent a /k/ sound – thus *k-ni-kt*. For further practice, please see the 'Spelling patterns and letter strings' section in the Year 6 workbook.

In this chapter

Rules and exceptions page 47	To spell words with the /ee/ sound spelled 'ei' after 'c'.
A tricky letter string page 51	To spell words containing the letter string 'ough'.
Silent letters page 55	To spell words with silent letters.
Assessment page 59	Activities and ideas to assess knowledge and use of spelling patterns and letter strings.

Poster notes

Spelling patterns and silent letters (page 46)
Use the poster as a reference to show children how the pronunciation of words with the same letter string can be quite different. Reinforce the exceptions to the rule for *i before e*. How many words with silent letters can they think of before the bottom section of the poster is revealed?

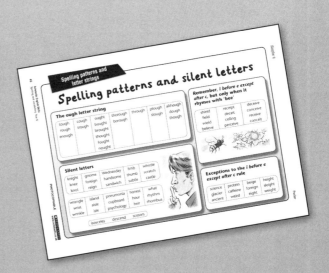

Spelling patterns and letter strings

Spelling patterns and silent letters

Remember, i before e except after c, but only when it rhymes with 'bee'

shield	receipt	deceive
field	deceit	conceive
wield	ceiling	receive
believe	perceive	conceit

Exceptions to the i before e except after c rule

science	protein	beige	height
glacier	caffeine	foreign	sleight
ancient	weird	eight	weight

The ough letter string

tough	cough	ought	thorough	through	plough	although
rough	trough	bought	borough		slough	dough
enough		brought				though
		thought				
		fought				
		nought				

Silent letters

knight	gnome	Wednesday	limb	whistle
knee	foreign	handsome	thumb	scratch
knot	reign	sandwich	subtle	castle

wrangle	island	pneumonia	honest	what
wrist	aisle	cupboard	hour	rhythm
wrinkle	isle	psychology	heir	rhombus

isosceles	descend	scissors

■SCHOLASTIC
www.scholastic.co.uk

Rules and exceptions

To spell words with the /ee/ sound spelled 'ei' after 'c'.

Background knowledge

The *i before e except after c* rule is well known, but the spelling convention relies on the sound produced by the digraph. For words that contain a long /ee/ sound, 'ie' is the convention except when it comes after 'c' – for example, *receive*. The children will note that the rule applies when the sound in these words is /ee/. Where it is **not** /ee/, the rule has exceptions. Words containing a long /ai/ sound can use 'ei', such as *freight*, *weight and beige*. Other exceptions to the rule, which children need to learn, include *science*, *glacier* and *ancient*.

Learning the general rules of spelling draws children's attention to their exceptions. If children are encouraged to discover rules themselves through investigation, they will be far more likely to remember the rules and exceptions.

Activities

● **Photocopiable page 48 'Which order?'**
In this activity the children use a dictionary to add words to three columns: words that use the *i before e* pattern; words that use 'ei' following 'c'; and words that are exceptions to the *i before e* rule. As they add words to each column, encourage them to find their own rule to explain the spelling patterns. Check that they are categorising the words in the correct way. Help the children to note that the rule applies when the sound in these words is /ee/ – where it is not /ee/, the rule has exceptions.

● **Photocopiable page 49 'Rule or exception?'**
Invite the children to come up with a list of as many words as possible that contain one of the two vowel digraphs 'ie' or 'ei'. Establish the sound made by each digraph. Consider that when the sound is /ee/, the 'i' comes before the 'e' except after 'c' (with a

few exceptions). Invite them to sort out such words. Reinforce the fact that when the vowel digraph makes any other sound, such as /ai/, the rule does not apply. The children then sort the words in the word pool into their correct spelling rule category.

● **Photocopiable page 50 'Should I use ie or ei?'**
Before starting the crossword, revise the rules and exceptions with the children. Call out different words with both 'ei' and 'ie' spellings that make a number of different sounds and ask the children to write, on whiteboards, either 'ei' or 'ie' (but not the whole word), so that any misconceptions can be addressed before starting the activity.

Further ideas

● **Spelling mobiles:** Set up vowel-sound mobiles to be hung from the ceiling. Suggest that the children word-process good examples of 'ie'/'ei' words they discover during reading or class research in other curriculum areas to add to the mobiles.
● **Shared and independent reading:** As the children read with the class, and independently, encourage them to collect exceptions to the known spelling rules.
● **Rule of the day:** Choose a spelling rule each day and challenge the children to find words that prove the rule.

Digital content

On the digital component you will find:
● Printable versions of all three photocopiable pages.
● Answers to 'Rule or exception?' and 'Should I use ie or ei?'.
● Interactive version of 'Rule or exception?'.

Name:

Which order?

■ Use a dictionary to find and add words with the letter strings **ie** and **ei** to these three columns. Compare the words you have written in the first and middle columns. What pattern can you find?

i before e	e before i after c	exceptions – e before i without a c
piece believe	ceiling receive	foreign weird

■ Write the rule and its exceptions here and add them to your spelling journal.

_____

_____

PHOTOCOPIABLE

Rules and exceptions

Rule or exception?

■ Sort the words in the word bank into the correct boxes using the rule *i before e except after c when the sound is /ee/*. Identify words that are exceptions to this rule – and learn them.

Words that have an ie spelling making an /ee/ sound, with no c	Words that have an ei spelling making an /ee/ sound, following a c

ceiling   deceit   achieve   yield   conceited

caffeine   receipt   grief   perceive   beige   neither   shriek

                  field   piece   handkerchief   weird

siege   thief   seize

belief   fierce   brief   either   niece   shield

                  receive   protein

Exceptions to the rule

Name:

Should I use ie or ei?

■ Work out the answers to the clues to complete the crossword. Each answer contains either the **ei** or **ie** spelling pattern.

Across

6. To force a hole through something.
9. Grassy area found in the countryside.
10. Strange or unfamiliar; not from one's own country.
11. To become aware of something.
13. A female family relative.
14. Extremely proud of oneself; vain.
16. A creamy brown colour.
18. To grab hold of.

Down

1. Essential for a healthy diet.
2. To provide protection.
3. To successfully reach a desired result.
4. Aggressive or angry.
5. A stimulant found in tea and coffee plants.
7. An operation to surround an area and cut off supplies.
8. The top of the room.
12. Trust or faith in something or someone.
15. A part of something.
17. A utensil for separating solids from liquids.

■ SCHOLASTIC
www.scholastic.co.uk

A tricky letter string

Objective

To spell words containing the letter string 'ough'.

Background knowledge

The letter string 'ough' can be tricky to spell, especially as it can be used for a number of different sounds. For example, *enough*, *although*, *cough*, *through* and *thorough* all have the 'ough' letter string but are pronounced differently. Although these words just have to be learned, children will find mnemonics are useful strategies for creating a visual and oral basis to remember these tricky spellings. They are very powerful when they are used for a group of words, in that they can represent the tricky bit of a word family.

Activities

● **Photocopiable page 52 'Fun with mnemonics'**
Before starting the photocopiable sheet, children can think of their own mnemonics for the 'ough' letter string and then choose their favourite to write in their word bank book/spelling book. Ask the class to vote for the best/funniest appropriate mnemonic. Look at the words at the bottom of the photocopiable sheet together. Ask the children to say what they notice about the pronunciation of the words. They should sort and write the words next to the appropriate 'hunks', according to how each word is said.

● **Photocopiable page 53 'What's my spelling?'**
This photocopiable sheet encourages the children to consider the different *sounds* of words containing the letter string 'ough'. Revise beforehand the different sounds to help them work out the correct spellings of the two incorrectly spelled words in each sentence. This should then aid them in completing the table at the bottom of the photocopiable sheet.

● **Photocopiable page 54 'Sort it'**
Let the children have fun with creating sentences containing two words that rhyme, giving examples if necessary. They don't have to make complete sense. The task at the bottom of the photocopiable sheet likewise can be more about the children having fun with words than accuracy of sense.

Further ideas

● **More mnemonics:** Invite the children to create mnemonics for other common tricky letter strings, such as 'igh'.
● **Word families:** Extend the work on 'ough' letter strings to other words in the same word families – for example, *rough/roughness/roughly* and *thought/thoughtful/thoughtless*.
● **Silly spellings:** Ask the children to write phonetically on whiteboards words that you call out containing the 'ough' letter string. Then they can share each word with a partner and together work out the correct spelling. For example, they may write *tuff* and then work in pairs to spell it accurately as *tough*.

Digital content

On the digital component you will find:
● Printable versions of all three photocopiable pages.
● Answers to all three photocopiable pages.
● Interactive versions of 'Fun with mnemonics' 'What's my spelling?'.

Name:

Fun with mnemonics

■ A great way of remembering the spelling of **ough** words is to use a mnemonic. Look at this one: *Oh U Gorgeous Hunk*! Think of your own mnemonics for **ough**, then choose your favourite and write it in the box below. Be prepared to share it with the rest of your class.

My **ough** mnemonic:

■ The tricky hunks below all say the **ough** letter string differently. Look at the words at the foot of the page and sort them into rhyming groups above the names of the relevant hunks.

_____

_____

| Tough Ted | Peter Plough | Dan Dough |

_____

_____

| Olly Ought | Troy Trough |

thought	trough	rough	slough	sought
plough	fought	cough	although	
enough	tough	bough	though	

A tricky letter string

What's my spelling?

■ Two words in each of these sentences have been spelled as they sound – but they should all contain the **ough** letter string. Find the incorrect words and then rewrite them correctly on the lines below.

I thawt my mother had bawt me some sweets to cheer me up.

_____   _____

But she brawt me some coff medicine instead.

_____   _____

Althow my brother and I fawt sometimes, he could be very kind.

_____   _____

I was surprised when he brawt home a ruffly-wrapped package.

_____   _____

He had heard I had a bad coff and that I was thorully miserable.

_____   _____

He had bawt me some sweets even thow I hadn't asked him!

_____   _____

■ Complete the table below with as many words as you can think of that contain the letter string **ough**, matching them to the sounds in the column headings.

long o sound /oa/	/or/ sound	/uh/ sound	short /o/ sound	/ow/ sound

Name:

A tricky letter string

Sort it

■ Draw a line from the words on the left to those on the right to make rhyming pairs. Then write a sentence that contains each rhyming pair. One has been done for you.

enough	thought
although	borough
bought	trough
thorough	rough
bough	though
cough	slough

I'd had just about enough of these rough seas.

_____

_____

_____

_____

■ Can you use all of the words above that contain the **ough** letter string in one passage? Write it in the box below.

PHOTOCOPIABLE   **■ SCHOLASTIC**
www.scholastic.co.uk

Silent letters

Objective

To spell words with 'silent' letters.

Background knowledge

Silent letters in words can make spellings tricky. Children need to learn these words, and it can help them if they say each sound when practising their spelling. Stressing the silent letter can help them remember – for example, pronouncing the 'k' when saying *knock*, or the 'b' in *comb*.

Remind children that an apostrophe used for contraction is placed where a letter is omitted, and thus is effectively a silent letter – for example, *hasn't* for *has not*, where the apostrophe indicates the missing (or silent) 'o'.

Point out some patterns to the children: silent 'k' is always at the beginning of a word and has an 'n' after it; silent 'g' is followed by an 'n'; silent 'h' likes to be partnered with other letters, especially 'w' and 'r', such as *white* and *rhombus*; silent 'b' is almost always at the end of words as part of the grapheme 'mb' – for example, *limb;* silent 'l' (in the same syllable) comes between 'a' and 'k', 'a' and 'f', 'a' and 'v', 'a' and 'm', 'o' and 'k' and before 'd'; silent 'd' comes before a consonant – for example, *sandwich*; silent 'n' usually follows an 'm', such as in *autumn* (though observe the word *government*); silent 'p' is usually at the beginning of a word, often of Greek or Latin origin; silent 's' comes before an 'l', for example, *island*; silent 't' comes after an 's', such as *whistle*; and silent 'c' comes after an 's' – for example, *scissors*.

Activities

● **Photocopiable page 56 'Words with silent letters'**

Before beginning the activity, ask the children to list words they know that contain silent letters. In the activity, children answer clues to spell words with silent letters and practise their spelling using 'Look, Say, Cover, Write, Check'. Encourage the children to say each answer aloud and pronounce the silent letter as they speak the word.

● **Photocopiable page 57 'What's missing?'**

Display the poster on page 46 again and recap on silent letters and how the example words are pronounced. Work through the sentences on this photocopiable sheet, prompting the children to stop after each one to ask themselves which words look odd and why. What might the missing silent letters be in each 'odd' word? Encourage children to try different letters until they are confident they have found the right one.

● **Photocopiable page 58 'Find my silent letter'**

Ask the children to identify silent letters in words in the context of a piece of descriptive writing. They can then progress to using other words with silent letters in their own creative writing.

Further ideas

● **Silent letters:** List silent letters as column headings (for example, 'p', 'b', 'w', 'h', 'k') on a large piece of paper that is displayed prominently, and ask the children to add words that use each silent letter in the relevant columns.

● **Nonsense words:** Write a passage similar to that on photocopiable page 58 but leave out the silent letters. Ask the children to identify the words where silent letters have been omitted and to rewrite these words correctly.

Digital content

On the digital component you will find:
● Printable versions of all three photocopiable pages.
● Answers to all three photocopiable pages.
● Interactive version of 'What's missing?'.

Name:

Silent letters

Words with silent letters

■ The answers to these clues are all words with silent letters. Write the answers and circle the silent letter. Then practise spelling them using Look, Say, Cover, Write, Check. As you practise, say each letter sound aloud.

This person keeps people or places safe.   g __ __ __ d

You can cut paper with these.   s __ __ __ __ __ s

Joint between your hand and arm.   __ r __ __ t

A serious illness of the lungs.   __ n __ __ m o n __ a

To make this noise, purse your lips
and blow.   w__ __ __ __ __ e

A triangle with two equal sides.   i __ __ s __ __ __ __ s

You need these to move your bones.   m __ __ __ __ __ s

Give up a job.   r __ __ __ __ n

You do this with your ears.   l __ __ __ __ __

A large, edible, pink fish.   s __ __ __ __ n

Joints in the fingers.   __ n __ __ __ __ __ __

A quadrilateral with sides the same length.   r __ __ __ __ __ s

A regular beat.   r __ __ __ __ m

A machine for transporting people or cargo.   v __ __ __ c __ e

Our surroundings, including living and
non-living things.   e __ __ __ r __ __ __ __ n __

Silent letters

What's missing?

■ In each of the sentences below, there are two words with missing silent letters. Find the words and then write the correct spelling on the lines below each sentence.

After such a warm start to the autum, I dout that the winter will be very cold.

_____   _____

To the best of my nowledge, my grandmother is recovering well from a nasty bout of neumonia.

_____   _____

The fisherman was quite solem as he reeled in his catch – a large samon.

_____   _____

The bespoke kitchen contained cuboards with fluoresent lighting.

_____   _____

Today in maths we drew an isoseles triangle and a rombus.

_____   _____

I barely reconised the old woman with the narled fingers as my former teacher.

_____   _____

As the notes asended to a very high pitch, we struggled to hear the rythm.

_____   _____

My father is a sychologist but in his spare time he researches terodactyls.

_____   _____

With a great nashing of teeth, the gruesome nome returned to his cave.

_____   _____

Name:

Silent letters

Find my silent letter

■ Underline or highlight any silent letters you can find in the words in the paragraph below.

Mrs Knight likes baking bread. Last autumn, when I was visiting her, she showed me how to do it. I listened carefully to her instructions. I had to knead the dough for ten minutes. I used my knuckles but, even so, my wrists ached! Perhaps I was doing it the wrong way. I almost gave up because I knew I would never have the knack. Eventually, despite sore arm muscles, I had a lovely loaf of bread. The knife cut through it perfectly!

■ Highlight the silent letters in the words in the word bank below. Then write a paragraph using as many of these words as possible. An example of an opening sentence has been done for you. Use a separate piece of paper to write the passage on if necessary.

castle	foreign	caught	guard	knife
knight	could	night	ascended	listened
thistle	calm	twelfth	gnarled	doubtful
fight	thorough	sword	recognised	heir
descended	gnashing	glistened	handsome	scratch
signs	watched	might	wrestled	wretched

As the handsome knight ascended the mountainside to search for the stolen treasure, he watched and listened carefully for any signs that might spell danger...

_____

_____

_____

_____

Assessment

Assessment grid

The following grid shows the main objectives and activities covered in this chapter. You can use the grid to locate activities that cover a particular focus that you are keen to monitor.

Objective	Page	Activity title
To spell words with the /ee/ sound spelled 'ei' after 'c'.	48 49 50	Which order? Rule or exception? Should I use ie or ei?
To spell words containing the letter string 'ough'.	52 53 54	Fun with mnemonics What's my spelling? Sort it
To spell some words with 'silent' letters.	56 57 58	Words with silent letters What's missing? Find my silent letter

Observation and record keeping

While the children are completing the photocopiable sheets in this chapter, encourage them to keep a spelling journal to record how well they did and to note any difficulties encountered. Encourage them to write down words that were tricky for them. A note of appropriate rules, patterns and mnemonics will also be helpful to them. Use the spelling journals to provide evidence for assessing ongoing work. In the assessment activity, children's understanding of the *i before e* rule will be tested. They will also need to show knowledge of some 'ough' words and how they differ in meaning from their paired homophone. Finally, their ability to spell words containing the silent letters 'b', 's', 't', 'w' and 'h' will be assessed.

Assessment activity

● **What you need**
Photocopiable page 60 'Spelling tricky words'.
● **What to do**
Recap the spelling rule *i before e except after c* and go through some exceptions. Discuss the different sounds the letter string 'ough' makes and remind children what a homophone is. The children need to show they know the different meanings of each pair of words by writing appropriate sentences. Finally, they will have to unscramble anagrams to spell words containing silent letters.

Differentiation

● Less confident learners will benefit from a word bank of words with the 'ie' and 'ei' spellings. They should also have access to a dictionary for tasks two and three.
● More confident learners could extend the silent letters task to create their own anagrams and clues to the answers.

Further learning

● **Etymology:** Some children may be interested in the etymology of words that contain silent letters. For example, Old English *cniht* (meaning boy, youth or servant) is of West Germanic origin and is related to Dutch and German *knecht*.
● **Quick-fire activities:** How many words starting with silent 'k' (and so on) can the children think of? The children can write the words on their whiteboards.

Name:

Assessment

Spelling tricky words

■ Write three words that follow the rule *i before e*.

1 _____ 2 _____ 3 _____

■ Write three words that follow the rule *i before e except after c*.

1 _____ 2 _____ 3 _____

■ In these pairs of homophones, one word contains the letter string **ough**. Create sentences for **each** word to show their different meanings.

threw/through

_____

_____

doe/dough

_____

_____

bough/bow

_____

_____

ruff/rough

_____

_____

■ Unravel these anagrams to spell words that contain silent letters.

restwel _____

cumbusc _____

nladis _____

sitlouheet _____

Chapter 4

Word families, roots and origins

Introduction

The morphology of a word is how it is structured internally in terms of root words and suffixes or prefixes. There may be other changes – for example, irregular plural forms such as *mouse* to *mice*. This chapter focuses on the origins (Latin, Greek and French) of prefixes, suffixes and root words to extend the children's etymological knowledge and vocabulary. Decoding the discrete elements of complex words through etymology and morphology provides a strategy to help children to spell independently and understand many complex or extended words. Morphology may be used to produce different inflections of the same word, both belonging to the same word family – for example, *child, children*, or to build entirely new words such as *child, childhood*. For further practice, please see the 'Word families, roots and origins' section in the Year 6 workbook.

In this chapter

Poster notes

Word building (page 62)
The poster focuses on one root word of Latin origin, *port*, meaning to carry, bring or bear, and how it can be changed by adding different prefixes and suffixes. There are lots of activities that you could initiate using the poster: ask the children to experiment by adding a prefix to make a new word, such as *teleport*, adding a suffix, for example *portable*, or adding a prefix and a suffix, such as *transportation*. Encourage the children to add other root words and experiment with using the prefixes and suffixes to create word families. Provide the children with sticky notes to add other prefixes and suffixes to use with the root words as they work through the chapter.

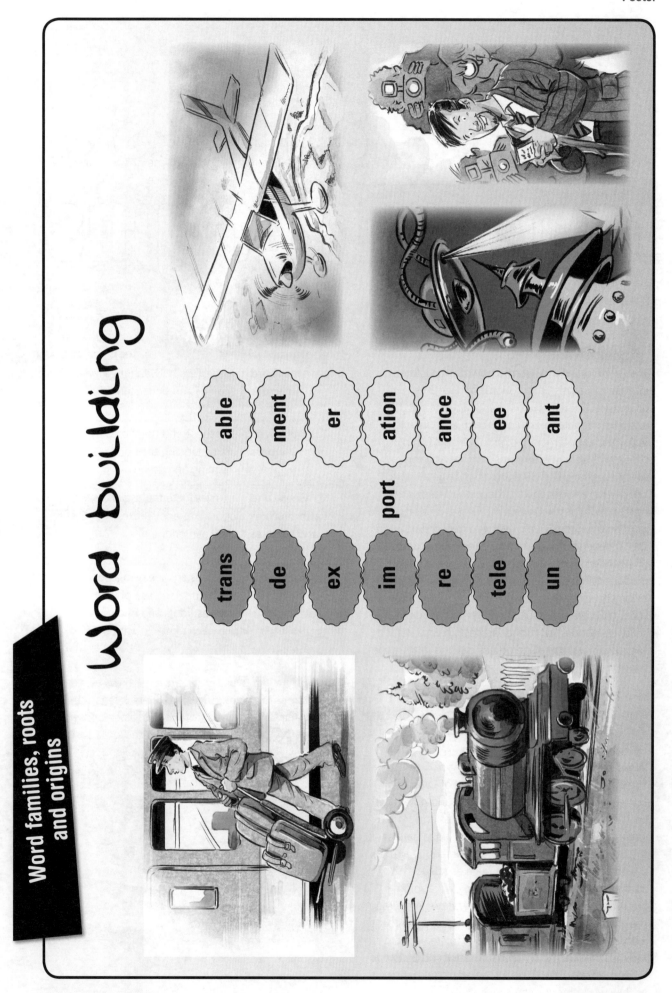

Word building

Word families, roots and origins

Word structure

Objective

To spell words with inflectional endings and understand the origin of words.

Background knowledge

Inflectional endings are suffixes that, when added to root words, alter the case, number, meaning or tense. Care needs to be taken when adding a vowel suffix to a root word that ends in 'e' or 'y': words ending in 'y' drop the 'y' when adding 'ed', 'er' and 'est' and replace it with 'i', and keep the 'y' when 'ing' is added. For most nouns ending in 'y', the 'y' is replaced by 'ies' in the plural, but observe exceptions: nouns ending in double 's' get 'es' in the plural; and words of Greek and Latin origin have different rules again.

A portmanteau is a travelling case made up of two halves, joined together by a hinge. It is also made of two words: the French *porter* (to carry) and *manteau* (a cloak). Portmanteau words are generally formed by joining the beginning of one word with the ending of a second, the two words having a common vowel. They were coined by Lewis Carroll in 1872. They are easily understood and are an easy way of creating new words.

Activities

● **Photocopiable page 64 'Crossword'**
The children are given single-word clues (verbs and adjectives) to help them fill in a crossword. They have to choose between the past tense 'ed' ending or the continuous 'ing' ending for verbs ending 'e' or 'y' (except for *go*) and 'er' or 'est' for adjectives, most of which end in 'y'. They will find counting the letter spaces in the crossword will help them to work out which ending to use. In a plenary session, ask the children what spelling patterns they noticed in these words when the suffixes were added. Together, generate a spelling rule for adding these endings. Find some

further examples that conform to the rule you have made. Can the children find any exceptions?
● **Photocopiable page 65 'Making plurals'**
In this activity the children change singular nouns into plural nouns and invent rules to help them remember how to pluralise nouns that end in 'y', and when to add 'es' and 's'. Finally, challenge them to make irregular nouns into plurals. Together, think of some ways to remember these tricky words. Create a display poster of tricky plurals that the children may add to as they come across them.
● **Photocopiable page 66 'Portmanteau words'**
Explain the origin of portmanteau words. If the children know any, invite them to work out which two words they originate from. Collect a few examples before inviting the children to complete the sums on the photocopiable sheet. During the plenary, check the spellings of the words and discuss why the children think some of the words were created.

Further ideas

● **Personal collections:** As the children engage in personal reading, ask them to collect words they meet that have unusual or tricky plural forms. Ask them to add words that drop 'y' when a suffix is added.
● **Portmanteau challenge:** Set the challenge of finding 50 valid portmanteau words. Award a prize for the most imaginative list. Award an individual prize for any group that finds an example that no one else found. (This will prevent them simply copying from websites.)
● **Portmanteau fun:** Challenge the children in pairs to 'invent' their own portmanteau words, albeit nonsense words. Start by giving them some suggestions of your own – for example, *amazing* + *wonderful* could be *amazeful* or, reversed, *wondermazing*.

Digital content

On the digital component you will find:
● Printable versions of all three photocopiable pages.
● Answers to all three photocopiable pages.
● Interactive versions of 'Making plurals' and 'Portmanteau words'.

Name:

Word structure

Crossword

■ Decide whether the clues given below are verbs or adjectives. Then add either **ed** or **ing** to the verb clues, and either **er** or **est** to the adjective clues, to fit them into the relevant spaces in the crossword grid.

Across

2. dance
3. take
4. ignore
6. place
10. deny
11. funny
13. easy
14. fly
15. early
16. go
17. wealthy

Down

1. sample
2. dry
5. calm
7. cry
8. reply
9. tiny
12. rage

■SCHOLASTIC
www.scholastic.co.uk

Word structure

Making plurals

■ Change these nouns to plural nouns:

key becomes _____

daisy becomes _____

donkey becomes _____

family becomes _____

city becomes _____

■ Look at the plural list and think of a rule to help you remember how to change singular words ending with **y** into plural words. Write your rule here.

_____

■ Change these words into plural words:

field becomes _____

box becomes _____

glass becomes _____

hutch becomes _____

fox becomes _____

■ Look at the plural list and think of a rule to help you know when to add **s** and when to add **es** to make a plural word. Write your rule here.

_____

■ Some plural nouns don't follow these rules. Write the plural of these nouns on a separate piece of paper and check them with a dictionary.

focus	crisis
woman	radius
goose	louse
larva	sheep
antenna	

SCHOLASTIC
www.scholastic.co.uk   **PHOTOCOPIABLE**   **Scholastic English Skills**
Spelling and vocabulary: Year 6   **65**

Name:

Word structure

Portmanteau words

In 1872, Lewis Carroll coined the term **portmanteau**: two words that are joined using the start of one word and the end of another. The two words usually have a common vowel that is often shared. In 1843, the word **squirl** was invented by blending together the words **squiggle** and **whirl** (to describe a flourish in handwriting).

■ Try to work out these portmanteau words by blending together the two original words. Can you make up some of your own?

electronic + mail = _____

prim + sissy = _____

breakfast + lunch = _____

motor + hotel = _____

guess + estimate = _____

parachute + trooper = _____

gigantic + enormous = _____

breath + analyser = _____

internal + communication = _____

outside + patient = _____

clap + crash = _____

fantastic + fabulous = _____

squirm + wiggle = _____

international + network = _____

blow + spurt = _____

bold + rash = _____

camera + recorder = _____

Borrowed words

To choose and use words by understanding their origin, meaning and usage.

Background knowledge

A word's etymology is its origins in earlier forms of English or other languages, and how its form and meaning have changed. Travellers have brought words from other languages into the English language throughout history and it is a living language that is constantly growing and changing. Many words that we accept as English vocabulary were borrowed from other languages during the Renaissance. For example, *anatomy* originates from French, *volcano* from Italian, *kiosk* from Turkish, *caravan* from Indian and *yacht* from Dutch. Other words are more obviously borrowed from other languages, such as *ballet* from French and *pizza* from Italian.

As well as whole words, English vocabulary borrows prefixes and suffixes from other languages, such as Latin and Greek. Understanding the meaning of Greek and Latin prefixes and suffixes will help children work out the meaning of many words in English. While it is not important or necessary for children to learn whether a prefix or suffix is Latin or Greek, they should recognise its meaning – for example, *aqua* (Latin) and *hydro* or *hydra* (Greek) all refer to water.

Encourage children to take an active interest in words and their meanings. Ask them to collect unusual and interesting words and use an etymological dictionary or encyclopaedia to find out more about them and to learn their use and spelling.

Activities

● **Photocopiable page 68 'Greek origins'**
Briefly explain to the children that our language has come from a lot of different sources, including Greek. Hand out the photocopiable sheet and explain that the children need to list as many words as they can think of that use each Greek word, using dictionaries to help with their spelling.

● **Photocopiable page 69 'Latin roots'**
Discuss how our language has words that come from a Latin origin. Hand out the photocopiable sheet and explain to children that they need to think of English words that are derived from the Latin words. Provide dictionaries to help the children with their spelling. Share some of the children's answers as a class.

● **Photocopiable page 70 'Foreign borrowings'**
Before beginning the activity, read aloud to the children the passage about chartering a boat for a sailing holiday in Greece and ask them to listen carefully for any words they think are borrowed from other languages. Invite the children to read the advertisement and identify the country of origin of the words in bold, using an etymological dictionary or internet access to help them.

Further ideas

● **Where in the world?:** Display a world map on the wall and encourage the children to use sticky notes to attach words to their country of origin. Add words to the map from independent reading during the week. Spelling homework could be to test the country names.
● **Magpie words:** Create a bar chart of different countries and colour in the columns when children discover new words borrowed from other languages. See which country has given English the most words. Include some of these words in spelling homework.
● **Personal dictionaries:** Children can create their own etymological dictionaries for words with origins other than English.

Digital content

On the digital component you will find:
● Printable versions of all three photocopiable pages.
● Answers to all three photocopiable pages.

Name:

Borrowed words

Greek origins

■ How many words can you think of that are derived from each of these Greek words?

Greek	Meaning	Words in English
agros	cultivated land	
autos	self	
bios	life	
gigas	enormous	
logos	word, reason	
monos	alone	
phobos	fear	
tele	far off	

■ Use five words derived from the Greek words above to complete this recount of a holiday on a Greek island.

When my friend was unable to come on holiday, it was a _____

decision to go alone. The island was small and I soon explored everywhere. There

was little _____ with only a few olive groves. One good thing was

the pool at the villa – it was _____ . Because it was so big, I could

swim for ages. However, later I developed a _____ about drowning

in it so I had to stop. As I was on my own, I _____ home almost

every day. It was good to talk to my family.

■ Write two sentences of your own using any English words that come from the other three Greek words in the list above.

_____

_____

PHOTOCOPIABLE   ■SCHOLASTIC
                                                                    www.scholastic.co.uk

Borrowed words

Latin roots

■ How many words can you think of that are derived from these Latin roots?

Latin	Meaning	Words in English
amare	to like, love	
annus	year	
aqua	water	
bene	well	
finis	end	
malus	bad	
portare	to bring, to carry	
sonare	sound	

■ Write a sentence for each of these adjectives that have a Latin origin.

amicable _____

annual _____

aquatic _____

beneficial _____

final _____

malicious _____

portable _____

resonant _____

■ Check the meaning of any unknown words in a dictionary.

Name:

Foreign borrowings

■   Which country do you think the words in bold originated from? Write the
word and its language of origin on another sheet of paper. Use a dictionary or the
internet to help you.

Sailing the Greek islands

We are a **family**-owned **company specialising** in **charters** aboard a fleet of
modern, well-**equipped yachts** in the Ionian Sea to the west of the Greek
mainland. The Ionian Sea, with its **crystal**-clear waters, gentle winds and many
beautiful islands, provides **safe** sailing for both **amateur** and **professional** sailors.
A **host** of attractions awaits you, from sheltered harbours and bays where you can
moor in comfort overnight, to beautiful islands to explore with **sites** of **historic**
and **mythological** interest, and **tavernas** where you can sample the local food
and soak up the **atmosphere**. For **novice** sailors, the southern Ionian region has
flat, calm seas where you are never more than an hour away from a sheltered
anchorage.

We provide charters for all levels. You can pick up your yacht, sail it yourself and
return it at the end, or we can provide you with a skipper who will do all the work
so you can just **relax** and enjoy your holiday. We also provide assisted charters,
where you can sail **independently** but within the **security** net of a **flotilla**.

Villas

If you want to combine a sailing holiday with time spent ashore, we have four
villas for rent. They are fully equipped with all modcons, **en suite** bathrooms,
heated swimming pools and a **veranda** for that evening drink as the sun sets over
the emerald sea. This can provide the ideal solution for groups with small children
and non-sailors.

Call us now on 087796 459030 to book.

PHOTOCOPIABLE   ■**SCHOLASTIC**
                                                                    www.scholastic.co.uk

Greek and Latin prefixes and suffixes

Objective

To investigate the use and spelling of prefixes and suffixes with Greek and Latin origins.

Background knowledge

English spelling borrows words, prefixes and suffixes from other languages, including Latin and Greek. An understanding of the meaning of Greek and Latin prefixes will help children to spell many words in English. For example, many words that begin with or contain the grapheme 'ph' are words that came from the Greek language. Knowing that many words have the Latin root *bene* (which means *well*) will help the children to recognise that several words such as *benefit, benevolent* and *benefactor* are spelled with a second 'e' that may be pronounced differently, and will also indicate that words containing this root have a positive meaning.

Activities

● **Photocopiable page 72 'Prefixes and suffixes'**
In this activity the children experiment with joining a Greek or Latin prefix to a Greek or Latin suffix to create new words. Encourage them to check their new words with a dictionary and practise spelling them using 'Look, Say, Cover, Write, Check'. Follow up the activity by playing a game with the whole class or a large group. Create prefix/suffix cards and provide each child with a card. The children need to find someone with a card that can be combined with theirs to make a word. For a further challenge, encourage the children to create imaginary words using one or more of the Greek and Latin roots. Can they also make up definitions for their imaginary words?

● **Photocopiable page 73 'Number prefixes'**
This activity introduces the children to prefixes commonly used to denote a number when associated with other nouns, adjectives and adverbs. Read through the recount with the children, stopping at each phrase

that contains a number to see if they can make links with words they know already – for example, *quad/quadrangle/quadrilateral* for four. Suggest that they underline the chunks of words or phrases that they think will help them to work out the meanings.

● **Photocopiable page 74 'New dictionary'**
Encourage the children to combine prefixes, word roots and suffixes to invent ten new words, before writing dictionary definitions for these words. Hold a short plenary session and invite selected children to choose one of their invented words, challenging the others to give a definition; compare this with each selected child's definition and discuss the differences.

Further ideas

● **Card game:** Ask the children to lay some prefix and suffix cards face down on a table. Invite them to pick a card and use the prefix or suffix in a sentence. Using whiteboards, children need to spell correctly the word they have used in their sentence.

● **Your number's up:** Provide the children with a set of number words that use prefixes. Let them pick a card, read the word silently and then describe it to the class without using the actual word. The other children guess the word. Children need to spell each word correctly on whiteboards.

● **The big bluff:** Find unusual words that use Greek or Latin prefixes and suffixes and invent some new words as well. Select four children and give them a word each, one of which is invented, and a definition for each word. Ask the children to read out their words and definitions. The class vote for the word they think is invented. Repeat using four different children.

Digital content

On the digital component you will find:
● Printable versions of all three photocopiable pages.
● Answers to 'Prefixes and suffixes' and 'Number prefixes'.
● Interactive version of 'Prefixes and suffixes'.

Greek and Latin prefixes and suffixes

Prefixes and suffixes

■ Put these prefixes and suffixes together to make complete words. How many can you make?

■ Write them as a list at the bottom of the page. Check them in a dictionary and then practise spelling them using Look, Say, Cover, Write, Check.

Prefix	Suffix
photo	logy
archaeo	cycle
auto	phone
micro	scope
hemi	sphere
uni	graphy
tele	matic

Word list

PHOTOCOPIABLE   **■ SCHOLASTIC**
www.scholastic.co.uk

Greek and Latin prefixes and suffixes

Number prefixes

■ Change the phrases in bold in this recount into number-related words. Use a dictionary to help you. Write the new words on the lines below.

I cycled on my **three-wheeled bike** up to the gallery, walked across the

_____

square-shaped concrete area and went through the door. Inside was a

_____

hundred-year-old man who took my ticket. He peered at me through his

_____

two-lens glasses.

_____

"I haven't seen you for a long time," he said.

"No, it has been a **period of ten years** since I was here," I replied.

_____

I went into the main hall and there was a **group of four musicians** playing in

_____

the corner. I prefer them to the **group of five musicians** or the **two musicians**

_____   _____

I saw on my last visits. I noticed that the cellist wore a short-sleeved shirt that

showed off his strong **upper-arm muscles**.

_____

I sat on an **eight-sided** sofa in the centre and studied the paintings. I was

_____

particularly impressed by a picture of flowers. I think they are the sort that only

flower **every two years**.

_____

As I left, the old man said that he got quite bored taking the tickets.

"It's very **one-toned**," he commented, and joked, "the visitors are okay, but really I

_____

prefer **four-legged animals**!"

_____

Name:

New dictionary

■   Invent ten new words by adding a prefix and a suffix to one of the word roots below.

■   Write your words in a list and add a dictionary-style definition. The first one has been done for you.

Prefix	Word root	Suffix
aero	phon	hood
super	anim	ic
pro	bio	ation
sub	funct	ment
hyper	port	dom
tele	cred	oid
trans	spher	aphy

aerportoid   (adjective)   having the shape of an airport

_____   _____   _____

_____   _____   _____

_____   _____   _____

_____   _____   _____

_____   _____   _____

_____   _____   _____

_____   _____   _____

_____   _____   _____

Assessment

The following grid shows the main objectives and activities covered in this chapter. You can use the grid to locate activities that cover a particular focus that you are keen to monitor.

Objective	Page	Activity title
To use knowledge of morphology and etymology in spelling.	64	Crossword
	65	Making plurals
	66	Portmanteau words
	68	Greek origins
	69	Latin roots
	70	Foreign borrowings
	72	Prefixes and suffixes
	73	Number prefixes
	74	New dictionary
To use further prefixes and suffixes and understand the guidelines for using them.	72	Prefixes and suffixes
	73	Number prefixes
	74	New dictionary

Observation and record keeping

While the children are completing the photocopiable sheets in this chapter, encourage them to keep a spelling journal to record how well they did and to note any difficulties encountered. Encourage them to write down words that were tricky for them. A note of appropriate rules, patterns and mnemonics will also be helpful to them, together with a reminder of the word's origins and any related words or words with a similar grapheme–phoneme correspondence. Use the spelling journals to provide evidence for assessing ongoing work. Note that visual and kinaesthetic memory are more important to some children than others, so recognise and praise any alternative or creative strategies in their journals and encourage them to share them with the class.

Assessment activity

● **What you need**
Photocopiable page 76 'It's all Greek to me', writing materials.
● **What to do**
Children will use their knowledge of Greek and Latin prefixes to locate words in the word search. To challenge the children, they will write sentences – on a separate sheet – containing each word they find. In the second activity, the children will consider the meaning of number prefixes in Greek and Latin and how these can help them work out the meanings of words.

Differentiation

● Less confident learners may need access to a dictionary to complete the tasks. To support them with the word search, highlight the first letter of each word. To complete the table with the number prefixes, give less confident learners definitions of words that start with trickier prefixes (take these from this task's entry in the 'Answers' section on the CD-ROM), to enable them to work out the related number meaning. Consequently, they would not then complete the third column.

Further learning

● **Greek or Latin:** Encourage the children to think carefully about words with Greek or Latin prefixes and suffixes when reading and writing in other areas of the curriculum, for example maths or geography. How many words ending in 'ology' can they think of?
● **Independent writing:** Provide the children with a list of some of the words from the photocopiable sheets in this chapter and challenge them to write them into a paragraph or a sentence.

Name:

Assessment

It's all Greek to me

■ Find the ten Greek and Latin words hidden in this word search.

m	e	p	o	c	s	e	l	e	t
h	p	a	r	g	e	l	e	t	d
t	e	l	e	p	a	t	h	i	c
t	r	i	c	y	c	l	e	a	d
d	y	g	o	l	o	i	b	f	c
c	i	t	e	m	h	t	i	r	a
p	h	o	t	o	g	r	a	p	h
p	n	e	u	m	a	t	i	c	k
a	u	t	o	g	r	a	p	h	c
c	i	r	t	e	m	o	e	g	g

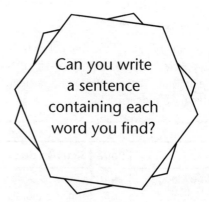

Can you write a sentence containing each word you find?

■ What number do the following Greek and Latin prefixes relate to? Write a word starting with each prefix. The first two have been done for you.

Prefix	Number	Word
uni	one	universal
quart	four	quarter
hex		
mono		
du		
hept		
non		
tri		
dec		
di		
mill		
quin		
bi		
sex		
hemi		
oct		
semi		
quad		
cent		
penta		

Chapter 5

Tricky words

Introduction

The word 'homophone' is derived from Greek and means 'the same sound'. Homophones are words that sound the same when pronounced but have different spellings. There are many pairs of homophones, but there are also some groups of three or four words with the same pronunciation but different spelling. They are often confusing and can cause spelling errors. The trick is to remember which spelling goes with which meaning. Sometimes there is a slight difference in the sound of the word, such as *affect* and *effect*. These words are called 'near homophones' and can be difficult to spot because they rely on correct pronunciation. For further practice, please see the 'Tricky words' section in the Year 6 workbook.

In this chapter

Homophones and easily confused words page 79	To spell homophones and other words that are easily confused.
Spelling tricky words page 83	To understand that the spelling of some words needs to be learned specifically.
Strategies for spelling page 87	To use a range of strategies as aids to spelling longer or tricky words.
Assessment page 91	Activities and ideas to assess knowledge and use of tricky words.

Poster notes

Homophones (page 78)

This poster provides examples of homophones, near homophones and particularly tricky homophones. When reading through the poster with the children, discuss strategies to help them remember the spellings of the trickier words. They might choose mnemonics or other memory-joggers – whatever works for them. Suggestions are: *the principal is my pal*; *it's quite quiet in here*; *I won one game*. They might remember *advice/advise*, *licence/license*, *practice/practise* if they remember that the 'c' in the noun is closer to the letter 'n' (for noun) in the alphabet, whereas the 's' in the verb is closer to the letter 'v' (for verb) in the alphabet.

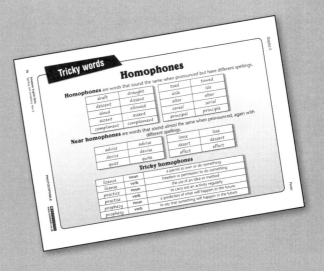

Tricky words

Homophones

Homophones are words that sound the same when pronounced but have different spellings.

draft	draught
descent	dissent
aloud	allowed
ascent	assent
compliment	complement

toad	towed
aisle	isle
altar	alter
cereal	serial
principal	principle

Near homophones are words that sound *almost* the same when pronounced, again with different spellings.

advice	advise
device	devise
quiet	quite

loose	lose
desert	dessert
affect	effect

Tricky homophones

licence	noun	a permit to own or do something
license	verb	freedom or permission to do something
practice	noun	the use of an idea or method
practise	verb	to carry out an activity regularly
prophecy	noun	a prediction of what will happen in the future
prophesy	verb	to say that something will happen in the future

Homophones and easily confused words

Objective

To spell homophones and other words that are easily confused.

Background knowledge

Many words in English are homophones – they have very similar sounds but different spellings. It can help children to differentiate between confusing pairs (or groups) of words when they investigate their meaning and use their own strategies for using them accurately. Looking for words within words can help, as can identifying the tricky part of one of the words and making up a rhyme, acrostic or other mnemonic about that bit. For example, the spelling of the words *principle* and *principal* is often confused. A mnemonic to help differentiate them might be: *The principal is my pal!* Or with the words *stationary* and *stationery,* the 'e' reminds us of 'pen'. Children should also be aware of the word class of a word, as this can help with the spelling. Words that end with 'ce' are usually nouns (such as *practice, licence* and *advice*), while words ending in 'se' are usually verbs (as in *practise, license* and *advise*). Note that the American spelling of these words is the 'ce' ending for both nouns **and** verbs.

Other words that are not true homophones – sometimes called near homophones – are easily confused, such as *dessert* and *desert*.

Activities

● **Photocopiable page 80 'Know the meanings'**
In this activity the children write their own definition of homophones and near homophones, followed by the dictionary definition and a sentence that uses the word correctly in context. As a follow-up activity to help them to consolidate their knowledge, ask them to identify the words they find tricky and encourage them to write a memory-jogger or mnemonic to help them remember – for example, *the principal is my pal* as discussed with the poster notes. Suggest that they record these words and memory-joggers in their personal spelling journals.

● **Photocopiable page 81 'Crossword crazy'**
Children will need dictionaries and spare paper before writing onto the crossword grid or the clues section. This activity will further consolidate the different meanings and spellings of the homophones and near homophones they have encountered.
● **Photocopiable page 82 'Matching words'**
In this activity, children will match a homophone, or near homophone, to the words in the table. For some words there is more than one match – for example, *raise, rays, raze* and *pour, pore, poor*. It is important to note that some words are pronounced differently depending on regional accents, such as *our* and *are*.

Further ideas

● **Quiz:** Using pairs of homophones and near homophones, ask the children to choose three pairs of words each and create a class quiz. Each child writes a clue about one word's spelling and meaning for each of their three pairs of words. Pool their clues and hold a quiz. Provide the children with whiteboards and pens. Arrange them into small, mixed-ability groups to play against each other in a timed competition. Read some mnemonics aloud to the children without letting them see the written word. The group who all write the correct word on their boards in the shortest time wins.
● **Crossword crazy part 2:** Allow children to create more homophone crosswords, online this time, and post them on the school blog/website. Invite siblings and/or parents to complete the crosswords.

Digital content

On the digital component you will find:
● Printable versions of all three photocopiable pages.
● Answers to 'Matching words'.
● Interactive version of 'Matching words'.

Name:

Homophones and easily confused words

Know the meanings

■ Discuss the definition of each word with your partner and write what you think it is in the table, before checking it against the dictionary definition. Then, on a separate piece of paper, write sentences using each of the words.

Word	My definition	Dictionary definition
descent		
decent		
dissent		
vain		
vein		
vane		
stationary		
stationery		
ascent		
assent		
loose		
lose		
allowed		
aloud		
principal		
principle		

Crossword crazy

■   Create your own crossword where two different clues give homophones as their answers. The first two clues – and answers – have been done for you. Your challenge is to see if you can use a letter from one answer in the word for another answer.

	¹d	e	s	c	e	n	t								
	i														
	s														
	s														
	e														
	n														
	t														

Across
1. The climb down.

Down
1. Difference of opinion.

_____   _____

_____   _____

_____   _____

_____   _____

_____   _____

_____   _____

_____   _____

_____   _____

SCHOLASTIC
www.scholastic.co.uk   PHOTOCOPIABLE   Scholastic English Skills
Spelling and vocabulary: Year 6   81

Name:

Matching words

■ Write a matching homophone, or near homophone, for the following words.
There may be more than one answer for some words.

warn		isle	
paws		they're	
right		led	
morning		heard	
cereal		guessed	
whale		past	
root		practise	
pour		advice	
profit		complement	
flecks		loose	
seen		draft	
raise		desert	
alter		steel	
grown		who's	
seem		precede	
affect		father	
bridle		licence	
waist		tire	

Spelling tricky words

To understand that the spelling of some words needs to be learned specifically.

Background knowledge

Learning and using the technique of dividing words into syllables and sounds can help children learn the spellings of tricky words – for example, *sep-a-rate*. Practice in deconstructing and analysing the spelling conventions of these types of words will help children to work out the most plausible spelling of complex words. There are many words with vowels that are difficult to hear because they are spoken quickly or quietly. When the stress falls on one syllable and not another, the vowel in the unstressed syllable is often unsounded when spoken, for example, in the suffixes 'ary' and 'ory'. Also, the letter strings 'er' and 'ed' are frequently unstressed. The conventional way of dividing words into syllables is to include a vowel sound in each syllable and to split double letters. Breaking a word up into syllables with double letters and unstressed vowels, then pronouncing each syllable separately, will help children remember the correct spelling by giving them a visual and auditory image of the word.

Activities

● **Photocopiable page 84 'I say, I say, I say'**
The children are given a list of misspelled words where either an unstressed vowel or sound is missed out. Ask them to predict the missing letter before they use a dictionary to investigate. After the children have completed the activity, ask them to work with a partner and say each word out loud, stressing the unstressed letter (saying it as it is spelled) to reinforce the spelling.
● **Photocopiable page 85 'Write it right'**
Ask the children to solve the clues provided. The answers are all words with tricky spellings. Placing each letter individually into the grid will help them think about

each syllable and sound as they write. For less confident learners, write one or more letters in the grid for them so that they can use them to help work out the rest of the word.
● **Photocopiable page 86 'Sight and sound'**
In this activity the children are given a list of frequently misspelled words and tips to help them analyse each word, thus improving their ability to spell them accurately. When the children have completed the activity, hold a plenary session to discuss which words they found tricky, and why. What were the most frequent mistakes? Ask them to give their opinion about using the 'Look! and Say!' strategy and how (or if) it helped them to learn each spelling.

Further ideas

● **Spelling journals:** As the children encounter other words in their personal reading with the same letter strings, encourage them to add these words to their spelling journals.
● **Spelling mobiles:** Attach cards with tricky words written 'normally' (for example, *separately*), and on the flip side show the word divided up into syllables (*sep-a-rate-ly*) to encourage use of this technique in learning the spelling of tricky words.
● **What word am I?:** Ask the children to write words as they might be spelled phonetically – for example, *veeickle* (*vehicle*), and ask their shoulder partner to guess the word and then attempt to spell it correctly. There is no right or wrong with their 'phonetic' spellings. They could have fun doing something similar with their own names as a warm-up. Use dictionaries to support their spelling.

Digital content

On the digital component you will find:
● Printable versions of all three photocopiable pages.
● Answers to 'I say, I say, I say' and 'Write it right'.
● Interactive version of 'I say, I say, I say'.

Name:

Spelling tricky words

I say, I say, I say

Some words have syllables or sounds that are not pronounced. One strategy to help you spell these words is to split the word up so that you pronounce each syllable and sound separately – for example, *sep-a-rate-ly*.

I say:

I write:

BUT

■ A letter is missing in each of the words below. Can you work out what it is? Use a dictionary to check. Then write out the correct word, separating it out into syllables.

parlament _____

necessry _____

accompny _____

enviroment _____

avrage _____

cemetry _____

defnite _____

desprate _____

dictionry _____

marvllous _____

privlege _____

PHOTOCOPIABLE

Spelling tricky words

Write it right

■ Use the clues to find the missing words in each grid. The unpronounced syllable or sound belongs in the shaded box in each case.

A measure of hot or cold

A type of transportation

A special entitlement

The body formed by the Queen, the House of Lords and the House of Commons

A place to eat out

Seven before the nineteenth

A plant mainly consumed by humans

SCHOLASTIC
www.scholastic.co.uk   **PHOTOCOPIABLE**   Scholastic English Skills
Spelling and vocabulary: Year 6   **85**

Name:

Spelling tricky words

Sight and sound

■ These words can be tricky to spell.

accommodation

symmetrical

exaggerate

audience

potential

burial

conscience

pronunciation

courtesy

ocean

queue

committee

mischievous

temperature

hindrance

possession

column

interrupt

government

physical

Look!

Look at the shape of these words one at a time. Make a picture of the word in your mind's eye. Look at the letters that make each of the sounds. Chunk the word into syllables. Find any words within words.

Say!

Say the whole word aloud. Say each syllable aloud. Say each sound in the word aloud. Say each sound, including silent letters, aloud. Say each letter name aloud. Say the word again.

■ Now cover up the words in the list and practise spelling them on a separate piece of paper.

■ Rewrite any that you got wrong and underline the part where you made a mistake, then follow the Look! and Say! steps again.

Strategies for spelling

Objective

To use a range of strategies as aids to spelling longer or tricky words.

Background knowledge

In this section, the children will be helped to spell tricky or frequently misspelled words by encouraging them to analyse what is tricky about the word, and then consider how best to learn the spelling. It will help if they can think of other words with related meanings or similar letter patterns. Encouraging the children to get a picture of the word in their mind's eye will help them to try out different spellings to see which one looks right. Mnemonics and memory-joggers are fun strategies to support spelling of such words. Acrostic mnemonics (a phrase or sentence made from the initial letters of the words) work well if they are unusual or humorous. Encourage the children to illustrate the acrostic in their mind's eye and to draw the picture next to their invented acrostic. If children make up their own mnemonics they are more likely to remember them.

Activities

● **Photocopiable page 88 'Now I remember'**
The children must find a shorter word within ten longer words, and then write their own memory-jogger or mnemonic using the short word to help them spell the longer word. Before beginning the activity, look together through the words on the photocopiable sheet and ask the children to suggest which parts of the words are the tricky bits that they could get wrong. Explain that if they can find a word in the tricky bit for their mnemonic, it will help them remember it. For example, a mnemonic that uses *out* will not be particularly helpful when spelling *outrageous* but *rage* would be very helpful, so, for example, *rabbits, ants, geese, elephants* might be a useful mnemonic, or *I go into a rage each time she behaves in an outrageous manner* might serve as a memory-jogger.

● **Photocopiable page 89 'Divide and conquer'**
Understanding and using the technique of dividing words into syllables and sounds can help children learn the spellings of tricky words. The conventional way of dividing words into syllables is to include a vowel sound in each syllable and to split double letters. Breaking a word up into syllables and then pronouncing each syllable separately will help children remember the correct spelling by giving them a visual and auditory image of the word.

● **Photocopiable page 90 'What are they?'**
In this activity the children are asked to make up memory-jogging acrostics to help them spell words with unstressed vowels and words containing silent letters.

Further ideas

● **Syllable cards:** Create syllable cards and ask the children to mix and match them to make words. Use dictionaries to check spelling.
● **What's my word?:** Children tell their shoulder partner a mnemonic or memory-jogger they have made (as part of the activity on photocopiable page 88). The partner must write the letters of each mnemonic on a whiteboard and see how quickly they can guess the actual tricky word.
● **Finding short words:** Challenge the children to find as many short words in a longer word as possible. For example, the word *inoperable* has six short words within it. Can they find another word with more than six?
● **New words:** Provide the children with a short word, such as *ten*. Ask them to find as many new words that have the short word within it as possible – for example, *tension, attention, potential*.
● **Wall display:** Make a decorated wall display of long words, with any words within the words coloured and written in different styles.

Digital content

On the digital component you will find:
● Printable versions of all three photocopiable pages.
● Answers to 'Now I remember' and 'Divide and conquer'.
● Interactive version of 'Divide and conquer'.

Name:

Strategies for spelling

Now I remember

■ Find a word within each of these words and use it to write a memory-jogger or mnemonic to help you spell it. The first one has been done for you.

argument   short word _____gum_____

Don't ever have an argument about gum.

outrageous   short word _____

_____

vegetable   short word _____

_____

desperately   short word _____

_____

average   short word _____

_____

frantically   short word _____

_____

privilege   short word _____

_____

relevant   short word _____

_____

secretary   short word _____

_____

definitely   short word _____

_____

explanation   short word _____

_____

■ Now look at your spelling log and add mnemonics for the words you always find tricky. For example, *accommodation – a room with two cots and two mattresses* (two **c**s and two **m**s).

Strategies for spelling

Divide and conquer

■ Divide these words into separate syllables. Split any double consonants and be sure that each syllable contains a vowel sound.

■ Count the number of syllables in each word and write your answers in the boxes. The first one has been done for you.

Word	Divided word	Number of syllables
embarrass	em-bar-rass	3
exaggeration		
miscellaneous		
category		
conscience		
temperature		
lightning		
recommend		
communicate		
develop		
marvellous		
guarantee		
outrageous		
opportunity		
privilege		
environment		
apostrophe		

Name:

What are they?

■ Write your own memory-jogger acrostics for these words with unstressed vowels and silent letters. For example, *physical – put hysterical young siblings in classrooms at lunchtime.*

parliament

p _____

a _____

r _____

l _____

i _____

a _____

m _____

e _____

n _____

t _____

desperate

d _____

e _____

s _____

p _____

e _____

r _____

a _____

t _____

e _____

average

a _____

v _____

e _____

r _____

a _____

g _____

e _____

cemetery

c _____

e _____

m _____

e _____

t _____

e _____

r _____

y _____

vehicle

v _____

e _____

h _____

i _____

c _____

l _____

e _____

Assessment

Assessment grid

The following grid shows the main objectives and activities covered in this chapter. You can use the grid to locate activities that cover a particular focus that you are keen to monitor.

Objective	Page	Activity title
To continue to distinguish between homophones and other words which are often confused.	80 81 82	Know the meanings Crossword crazy Matching words
To understand that the spelling of some words needs to be learned specifically.	84 85 86 88 89 90	I say, I say, I say Write it right Sight and sound Now I remember Divide and conquer What are they?

Observation and record keeping

As the children work through the photocopiable sheets in this chapter, make a note of any common errors made in their spelling of homophones, near homophones and other tricky or easily confused words. Observe which children keep their spelling journal updated and how they use it to create mnemonics, acrostics and other memory-joggers. Share any of the children's interesting, humorous or catchy strategies with the rest of the class.

Assessment activity

● **What you need**
Photocopiable page 92 'Which one am I?'.
● **What to do**
In this activity, children will choose the correctly spelled homophone or near homophone from the word bank provided to complete the passage, using the correct word in context. The second part of the assessment requires them to show their understanding of pairs of words by putting them into context in the sentences they create.

Differentiation

● Support less confident learners by helping them think of strategies to support their spelling of tricky words.
● Allow less confident learners access to dictionaries to assist with the assessment tasks.
● More confident learners could create their own passage or sentences with missing homophones, for a shoulder partner to complete.

Further learning

● **Word games:** Play a range of word games and challenge the children to explore words – both in class and at break times. Spelling well can be fun as well as rewarding. Play word snap, bingo and hangman, and create word searches and crosswords.
● **Oronyms:** Introduce children to homophones of multiple words or phrases known as 'oronyms', and let them have some fun with language. Examples are: *deep end/depend, four candles/fork handles, ice cream/I scream* and *example/egg sample*. Children can make up their own oronyms and swap with others to see if they can guess the alternative phrases.

Name:

Assessment

Which one am I?

■ Choose the correct word from the homophones below to complete the passage.

bare	scene	quiet	quite	allowed	slight	fare
sleight	effect	bear	aloud	seen	affect	fair

It didn't seem _____ that my friend was not _____ to read her

story _____. It was all about the _____ she had paid on the bus

to visit the local _____, and she was desperate to read it to the rest of the

class! However, the teacher had _____ her misbehaving on the playground

and, although she wasn't _____ making a _____, she was far

from _____. I couldn't _____ to see her upset but I had my own

troubles to _____: I had scraped my _____ legs on the rough wall

as I came in after lunch. The school nurse soon cleaned up my cuts and her good

care had a positive _____ on me. She said the antiseptic cream would not

_____ me other than a _____ sting. I clenched my teeth and, with

what seemed like a _____ of hand, she expertly rubbed it in before I was

aware what was happening!

■ Now write your own sentences to show you know the meanings of the
following pairs of homophones and easily confused words. Write one sentence for
each pair of words.

bridal	alter	compliment	advise	passed	stationary
bridle	altar	complement	advice	past	stationery

_____

_____

_____

_____

_____

PHOTOCOPIABLE

Chapter 6
Improving your work

Introduction

Children should be encouraged from an early age to self-edit and proofread their writing independently. Being able to use both a dictionary and thesaurus efficiently is crucial. There are many different ways children can improve their work: they can select more interesting vocabulary (in particular, adjectives, adverbs and verbs) by using a thesaurus to find *synonyms,* or words that mean the same or nearly the same. A thesaurus will also provide them with *antonyms,* or words that mean the opposite, which is helpful for spelling words with negative prefixes. Many thesauruses also provide words that relate to a particular topic. The ability to use a thesaurus effectively is a key tool in widening vocabulary and therefore assisting in improving writing standards. Additionally, children should be taught when it is appropriate to use formal or informal vocabulary. For further practice, please see the 'Improving your work' section in the Year 6 workbook.

Poster notes

Synonyms and antonyms (page 94)
The poster provides definitions and examples of synonyms and antonyms and can be used as a teaching tool while introducing the different activities in the chapter, or be produced as a large sheet for display purposes.

In this chapter

Dictionary skills page 95	To use a dictionary to check the spelling and meaning of words.
Synonyms and antonyms page 99	To find and use synonyms and antonyms to extend vocabulary and improve writing.
Using a thesaurus page 103	To use a thesaurus to find appropriate synonyms and antonyms.
Formal and informal vocabulary page 107	To understand the difference between vocabulary typical of informal speech as well as formal speech and writing.
Checking and improving writing page 111	To proofread for spelling errors and propose changes to vocabulary.
Bringing it all together page 115	To consolidate learning.
Assessment page 119	Activities and ideas to assess the improvement of work.

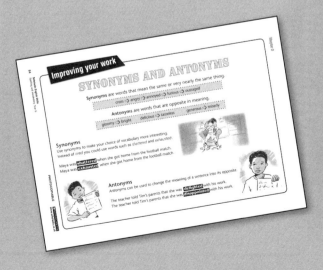

Improving your work

SYNONYMS AND ANTONYMS

Synonyms are words that mean the same or very nearly the same thing.

cross ⬄ angry ⬄ annoyed ⬄ furious ⬄ outraged

Antonyms are words that are opposite in meaning.

gloomy ⬄ bright   delicious ⬄ tasteless   generous ⬄ miserly

Synonyms

Use synonyms to make your choice of vocabulary more interesting.
Instead of *tired* you could use words such as *shattered* and *exhausted*:

Maya was **shattered** when she got home from the football match.
Maya was **exhausted** when she got home from the football match.

Antonyms

Antonyms can be used to change the meaning of a sentence into its opposite.

The teacher told Tim's parents that she was **delighted** with his work.
The teacher told Tim's parents that she was **disappointed** with his work.

Dictionary skills

To use a dictionary to check the spelling and meaning of words.

Background knowledge

It is important that children are taught how to use a dictionary efficiently. In the activities in this section, the children will use dictionaries to complete focused tasks in order to develop their understanding of the features and layout of a dictionary. There are a wide variety of dictionaries, at a range of levels. However, children should be introduced to the basic features and abbreviations used in the majority of cases. Draw their attention to how the class dictionary addresses:
- parts of speech (verb, noun, adverb, adjective, article)
- abbreviations
- meanings
- plurals
- antonyms and synonyms
- compound words
- derivatives.
    Dictionaries include information on the spellings of plurals and verb tenses, as well as providing help with pronunciation, which in turn can help with spelling. Children can use dictionaries to investigate root words and their derivatives, as well as the use of prefixes.

Activities

- **Photocopiable page 96 'Dictionary work'**
Children will practise using dictionaries in a variety of ways to find the information required for each of the three tasks. Being able to access words quickly and efficiently through knowledge of alphabetical order will encourage children to use dictionaries and thesauruses independently in their writing.

- **Photocopiable page 97 'Get to the root'**
Children will use dictionaries to create lists of derivations of words from given root words. Children should use the derivative words referred to in the specific entry for the root word, but they can also seek derivatives themselves by searching for subsequent entries on the dictionary page that use the same root word. Remind children that many words in the English language derive from Latin and Greek origin.
- **Photocopiable page 98 'What sort of word?'**
Children will find the list of words from the word bank in the word search and then use dictionaries to sort them into the correct word class. Before starting the activity, recap the different word classes – noun, verb, adjective and adverb – and confirm that the children know what each one is and what role each one has in a sentence.

Further ideas

- **Classy words:** Give the children a word such as *happy* and ask them to write on their whiteboards as many different derivatives of it as they can. Then discuss what word class each one is. When they get stuck, encourage further dictionary work to establish the class.
- **Quick dictionary:** Play a game where children in pairs use their dictionaries to find a given word. Give the children access to sticky notes. The winners are the first pair to hold up their dictionary with a sticky note under the given word.
- **Betwixt and between:** Give children two words that come quite close together alphabetically. On whiteboards, they need to write a noun, verb, adverb or adjective that comes between those two words.

Digital content

On the digital component you will find:
- Printable versions of all three photocopiable pages.
- Answers to all three photocopiable pages.

Name:

Dictionary skills

Dictionary work

■ Use a dictionary to find the definition and word class for each word.

Word	Definition	Word class
exemplary		
implore		
officious		
fragment		
avarice		

■ Use a dictionary to put the following groups of words into the correct alphabetical order. Write a number next to each word to show the correct order.

Group 1	Group 1	Group 2	Group 2	Group 3	Group 3
desperate		circumference		autobiography	
despair		circumspect		autograph	
destroy		circulation		autocratic	

■ Which word, from column A, B or C, will you **not** find in the dictionary *between* the words in the first column?

	A	B	C	D
filthy…finish	finally	fisherman	find	
break…breathe	breathless	breakfast	breast	
replenish…repulsion	report	replace	repulse	
accent…ascent	accident	ascension	ascertain	
offering…official	officious	office	officer	

Get to the root

■ Use your dictionary to find as many derivations as you can for each of the root words provided.

SIGN	JOY

LIKE	COMMAND

PRESS	FAVOUR

Name:

Dictionary skills

What sort of word?

■ Find the words in the word bank hidden in the word search. They may be vertical, horizontal, diagonal, forwards or backwards.

■ Use a dictionary to help you sort the words into each word class – noun, verb, adjective or adverb – then put them into the correct box below.

u	c	x	y	j	n	b	u	p	n	z	s	g	m	n
j	z	s	l	o	h	e	w	d	l	h	n	e	o	e
w	b	d	l	y	v	b	v	r	a	i	r	g	d	k
e	n	i	a	f	b	u	o	k	n	j	g	p	g	a
b	n	k	c	u	i	a	i	t	b	l	b	h	l	h
g	a	j	i	l	j	l	h	q	p	f	b	x	t	s
y	b	a	o	l	y	g	e	c	e	e	v	n	a	q
n	c	t	r	y	i	d	e	l	i	g	h	t	e	d
t	o	w	e	l	a	r	y	g	t	l	o	u	q	h
u	s	i	h	p	o	b	m	s	i	o	r	e	h	e
y	o	j	t	t	d	l	l	s	h	a	k	e	q	r
t	k	u	c	c	l	x	l	e	o	s	t	c	d	o
s	w	a	y	m	a	d	g	u	b	f	u	d	e	r
n	c	i	i	e	j	f	w	e	q	p	p	x	d	m
u	t	n	y	d	b	u	q	j	y	w	l	g	h	y

act
action
actor
hero
heroically
heroism
joy
enjoyable
joyfully
light
lightning
delighted
shake
shaken
shakily

Noun	Verb	Adjective	Adverb

PHOTOCOPIABLE

Synonyms and antonyms

Objective

To find and use synonyms and antonyms to extend vocabulary and improve writing.

Background knowledge

Synonyms are words that have the same meaning. However, many synonyms change meaning in different contexts – for example, in formal speech the word *children* may be used but in informal speech *kids*. Others reflect emotions, such as *youngsters,* which has a positive connotation, whereas *youths* can sound negative. Words such as *said* and *nice* are commonly overused words. To communicate more effectively what they mean, help the children to find more interesting alternatives that reflect what they really want to say. Many children choose weak verbs, such as *went*.

Antonyms are words with the opposite meaning. Some antonyms are easy to pair, such as *hot/cold and over/under*, but others work with several words. Many antonyms are made by adding a negative prefix to the root, such as 'dis', 'mis', 'un', 'il' and 'ir'.

Activities

● **Photocopiable page 100 'Synonyms and antonyms'**
Children will consider how they can make their writing more interesting and exciting by using different words for *said*. Extend the activity by asking the children to find synonyms for other words, such as *go* or *went*. They will also look at an editing task where the words and phrases used are not incorrect but simply not very adventurous choices. This should stand the children in good stead for editing and proofreading their own writing independently. Finally, they must choose antonyms so that the sentences in the third task make sense.

● **Photocopiable page 101 'Notes in class'**
Before starting this activity, read the poem aloud to the children. Invite them to describe what the poem is about. Ask them to listen for verbs in each stanza that tell them how the messages were written. When the children have completed the photocopiable sheet, invite them to use the synonyms they listed for the words in bold to write their own poem.

● **Photocopiable page 102 'Antonyms and opposites'**
Ensure that the children know that an antonym is a word meaning the opposite. One way to make words opposite is to use a negative prefix. Refer back to the work in Chapter 1 to demonstrate this. Recall prefixes that create opposite meanings and list them on the board. The children must match the words provided with the correct negative prefix and then use a thesaurus to check their choice. Challenge them to select a synonym for their newly made antonym.

Further ideas

● **Use it or lose it:** Collect any synonyms during the work carried out in this section. Distribute them among groups and challenge them to use each word in a sentence each time they speak to you.
● **Synonym trees:** Display three word trees around the class. When the children come across an unusual synonym for *nice, said* or *good* in their reading, ask them to write it on a leaf and stick it on the appropriate tree.
● **Synonym sack:** Put objects with different textures in a sack. In a circle, ask the first child to take an object and choose an adjective to describe it: *This flower is delicate*. Invite the next child to suggest a synonym of the adjective, such as: *This flower is fragile*. Ask the next child to think of a new adjective and the following child to give it a synonym. If a child 'passes' they can either use the thesaurus or ask the rest of the class for help.

Digital content

On the digital component you will find:
● Printable versions of all three photocopiable pages.
● Answers to all three photocopiable pages.

Synonyms and antonyms

■ Use a thesaurus to find synonyms for the word *said*. Two have been done for you.

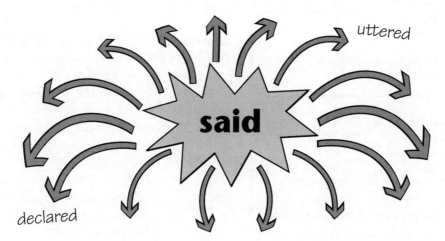

■ Make the paragraph below more interesting by replacing the words and phrases in bold with a suitable synonym. Remember to make them more powerful or exciting than the existing ones. Then rewrite the passage on the back of this sheet.

I **walked** down to the water's edge over the **hot**, **yellow** sand. The **feeling** of the **cold** sea **touching** my toes was **very nice**. In the distance, I saw a ship with **big** sails **sailing** across the horizon. I looked up at the **yellow** sun **shining** in the **blue** sky – it had been **shining** down on the sunbathers **non-stop** and some were starting to look **a bit red**. Time to go for a **nice swim**!

■ The following sentences will make more sense if you replace the words in **bold** with suitable antonyms. Rewrite the sentences on the back of the sheet.

My friend Joe is very **introvert**. Everywhere we go, he makes new friends and he is always the life and soul of the party.

The Greek gods were thought to be **mortal** beings who would live forever.

The pungent stench that made everyone heave was really **inoffensive**.

In a moment of **confusion**, the captain of the ship saw exactly what he must do to save the crew.

The engineers used a **flexible** material to strengthen the weak bridge.

Synonyms and antonyms

Notes in class

■ Find out how many times the verb **wrote** is used in the poem.
■ Think of different synonyms for the verb **wrote** each time it is used and write them below.
■ Write synonyms for the eight words and phrases in bold in the poem and write these below as well.

'You are like a red, red rose,'
he told her in his note.

'You are like a **slimy** slug,'
were the **cruel** words she wrote.

'My heart is yours **for ever**,'
he penned, 'forever true.'

'I would rather wash the dishes,'
she replied, 'than be with you.'

'You **smell** of summer flowers,'
he wrote, 'full blown and sweet.'

She wrote, 'You pong of sweaty socks
and even sweatier feet.'

He scrawled, 'My heart has **broken**
into pieces. I may die!'

She replied, 'Well why tell me,
I won't pretend I'd **cry**.'

He typed, 'My love has **turned** to hate.
My heart is now of stone.'

She scribbled, 'That's just typical.
I might have known you'd **moan**.'

Marian Swinger

Synonyms for the verb **wrote**:

_____

Other synonyms:

_____

_____

Name:

Antonyms and opposites

■ Select the correct negative prefix from the list to create an antonym for each starter word. Then think of a synonym for your antonym.

Negative prefixes	Starter word	Antonym	Synonym
im	agreeable		
	contented		
in	mature		
il	legal		
ir	appropriate		
	fortunate		
dis	moral		
un	advantage		
	regular		

Making antonyms

■ Create an antonym for each word in bold and write it on the line. Remember – don't just go for the first opposite word you think of; it must make sense.

Megan was **disappointed** _____ when she saw the **unsettled**

_____ weather.

We went full of **certainty** _____ to the fair as we had heard that the

world's **weakest** _____ man could barely **drop** _____ an

armchair above his head.

My teacher thought the film might be **appropriate** _____ for our age

group and therefore our parents might **approve** _____.

Mum said my handwriting was **legible** _____ and I should try to

prove _____ it or I would be **worthy** _____ of the

English prize.

Using a thesaurus

Objective

To use a thesaurus to find appropriate synonyms and antonyms.

Background knowledge

Using a thesaurus effectively can make more ambitious vocabulary accessible to children. A thesaurus provides alternative words with the same or similar meaning as the word being investigated: these are known as *synonyms*. A thesaurus also provides words with the opposite meaning to the focus word: these are called *antonyms*. A thesaurus, therefore, can assist with antonym spellings where negative prefixes are used. By looking up the word for which an antonym is required, children can identify whether they have used the correct spelling. Many thesauruses also provide words that relate to a particular topic.

The ability to use a thesaurus effectively is therefore a key tool in expanding vocabulary and improving writing standards. It is important that the children not only seek to use more interesting or powerful words but that they are also able to appreciate nuance, shades of meaning and connotation, and why one synonym may be more appropriate than another.

Activities

● **Photocopiable page 104 'The Lion and the Mouse'**
Aesop's Fables have been told for more than 2500 years. Show the children historical versions of the fables, such as Caxton's in 1484. Explain that, as language changes over time, there is a need for new adaptations. Ask them to rewrite a version of 'The Lion and the Mouse' for Key Stage 1 children. They should highlight any words that can be simplified and find alternative synonyms using a thesaurus or their own knowledge. Share the finished stories. Do they all convey the same meaning?
● **Photocopiable page 105 'Adventurous adjectives and astounding adverbs'**
Children should complete the photocopiable sheet using their thesauruses to identify useful and ambitious synonyms and antonyms for both the adjectives and adverbs listed. They can do this individually, in pairs or as a group. When completed, laminate the photocopiable sheets to be used as desktop vocabulary mats. Reward children who actively seek to improve their vocabulary.
● **Photocopiable page 106 'Wise words'**
Ask the children to find three synonyms for the highlighted word in each sentence and to identify which one is the most appropriate. This activity will assess how well children can use a thesaurus and select appropriate vocabulary. They will also realise that not all thesaurus entries can be used as straight replacements – there are shades of meaning that make vocabulary choice a precise art.

Further ideas

● **Create thesauruses:** Small notebooks can be made into thesauruses. Encourage the children to create an index at the front and head up each page with a number and keyword, such as *said*, *nice*, *good*, and so on. Hold short thesaurus sessions at the start of registration or at the end of the day, where children can record new words. Encourage them to record examples as they come across them in their reading.
● **Guided and independent reading:** Encourage children to consider more adventurous alternatives or synonyms to words they come across in their reading – ask the question: *What could the author have said to make the sentence more dynamic or powerful?*
● **Negative prefix challenge:** Write a list of negative prefixes: 'dis', 'mis', 'un', 'il', 'ir'. Hold a quick-fire session where children match given root words to the correct negative prefix to make its antonym.

Digital content

On the digital component you will find:
● Printable versions of all three photocopiable pages.
● Answers to 'Adventurous adjectives and astounding adverbs' and 'Wise words'.

Name:

Using a thesaurus

The Lion and the Mouse

■ Read this version of 'The Lion and the Mouse'.

■ Underline words that you feel are too advanced for a Year 1 or Year 2 audience and record them in the box below.

■ Use a thesaurus to find simpler synonyms for these words and then rewrite the story for a younger audience.

A lion was awakened from sleep by a mouse running over his face. Rising up in anger, he caught him and was about to kill him, when the mouse piteously entreated, saying: "If you would only spare my life, I would be sure to repay your kindness." The lion laughed and let him go.

It happened shortly after this that the lion was caught by some hunters, who bound him by strong ropes to the ground. The mouse, recognising his roar, came up, gnawed the rope with his teeth and, setting him free, exclaimed: "You ridiculed the idea of my ever being able to help you, not expecting to receive from me any repayment of your favour; but now you know that it is possible for even a mouse to confer benefits on a lion."

The moral of this story is, no one is too weak to do good.

Words from the story	Alternative, simpler synonym
awakened	woken up

PHOTOCOPIABLE

Using a thesaurus

Adventurous adjectives and astounding adverbs

■ Use your thesaurus to write synonyms and antonyms for these adjectives.

Adjective	Super synonyms			Astonishing antonyms	
beautiful					
happy					
marvellous					
angry					
strange					
calm					
annoying					
frightened					
loving					
miserable					
serious					

■ Use your thesaurus to write synonyms and antonyms for these adverbs.

Adverb	Super synonyms			Astonishing antonyms	
quickly					
carefully					
crossly					
wildly					
accidentally					
bravely					
anxiously					
sincerely					
finally					
deliberately					
carelessly					

Name:

Using a thesaurus

Wise words

■   Use your thesaurus to find three alternative words or phrases for those highlighted in **bold** in the text. Circle which one of the three you think is most appropriate.

1.   The doctor had been working through the entire night and was very **tired**.

_____   _____   _____

2.   Duncan did not attend school on Friday as he was feeling **ill**.

_____   _____   _____

3.   Sophie was very **happy** when her auntie came for a surprise visit.

_____   _____   _____

4.   The bomb disposal expert stayed perfectly **calm** as he disarmed the explosive device.

_____   _____   _____

5.   After she had finished her milk, the baby gurgled **happily**.

_____   _____   _____

6.   "Leave my brother alone!" shouted Harry **angrily**. "Go and pick on someone your own size!"

_____   _____   _____

7.   Half asleep, John **went** into the bathroom to wash his face and wake himself up.

_____   _____   _____

8.   The circus acrobats put on an **amazing** performance, which made the crowd gasp in anticipation.

_____   _____   _____

9.   Joe **walked** up the creaking staircase, holding his breath as he reached the last step.

_____   _____   _____

10. 'I'm really fed up with being in bed with this awful cold', **said** Brogan.

_____   _____   _____

Formal and informal vocabulary

Objective

To understand the difference between vocabulary typical of informal speech as well as formal speech and writing.

Background knowledge

In different times and places, language is used in different ways. When talking or writing to friends and family, we commonly use abbreviations, slang and colloquialisms, but in more formal contexts we use fewer abbreviations and seldom use slang or colloquialisms. We also change our language according to whether we are writing a formal or informal letter, email or text message. Although abbreviations pop up in text messages and email, they are not a new concept. *Bus*, *vet*, *fridge* and *IOU* are all abbreviations. In this section, children investigate how the medium in which they are writing and the degree of formality both influence their vocabulary choices.

Activities

● **Photocopiable page 108 'Can I join you?'**
Invite the children to read the informal request to join a skateboarding group and discuss the language used. Children will then write a formal request to join the school debating society/club, using words and phrases with the same meaning but that are more appropriate for a formal situation. Invite the children to read their paragraph aloud. Compare the two paragraphs and discuss which is the more persuasive, and why. Why do they think the first paragraph is more suitable for an informal situation and why do they think their own paragraph is more suitable for the school debating society?

● **Photocopiable page 109 'Text translation'**
Invite the children to read the text-message conversations and rewrite them as a telephone conversation between two friends. Then role play the messages as a telephone conversation, comparing how

the language changes and discussing the advantages and disadvantages of both.

● **Photocopiable page 110 'Believe me'**
Tell the children to write a letter to their teacher to explain why they were unable to complete a homework project. They should use formal language and be encouraged to use their dictionaries and thesauruses, as well as the word bank provided. Encourage them to compare the degree of formality in their language choices in all three activities from this section.

Further ideas

● **Achieve your goals:** Invite the children to work in small groups to make notes for a discussion on a subject, such as: *Play is more important than homework.* Ask groups to deliver their talks to the class. Discuss which groups used formal or informal language and what impact this had on their presentations. Invite the class to vote on which group was the most persuasive and why.

● **Formal or informal?:** Ask the children to list instances where it is more appropriate to use formal/informal language. Ask which they would use for the following: an email to a close friend; a letter to the prime minister; a text to a parent; their own personal diary; a letter to a sibling; or a persuasive speech about the environment.

Digital content

On the digital component you will find:
● Printable versions of all three photocopiable pages.
● Answers to all three photocopiable pages.
● Interactive version of 'Text translation'.

Name:

Formal and informal vocabulary

Can I join you?

■ Read this oral, **informal** request to join a skateboarding group. Then write your own oral, **formal** request to join the school debating society.

Hi, I'm Jack. I've seen you guys around here a lot. Looks like you have a really wicked time boarding! Can I join you? I'm an ace skateboarder – been doin' it years. I'd be a really cool guy to have in your gang. I could deffo demo some tricks. You wouldn't be sorry, I'd put money on it. So, what do you say? Am I in or what?

Good morning everyone. Allow me to introduce myself. My name is

_____

_____

_____

_____

_____

_____

_____

_____

_____

_____

Text translation

■ Translate the text messages below into a telephone conversation between two friends. When you have written the translation, role play the conversation with a partner.

Text speak	Phone speak
dnt 4get film 2nite. C U @ 6.	
Soz m8. Nt 2nite cus 2 much home wrk.	
2 bad. Gr8 riteup. Goin 4 pizza afta. Join us if U cn.	
Yeh if i cn. Spk ltr m8. Will gt maths done asap.	
OK. C U in pizza plce praps. Brng maths 2!	
LOL! ☺ Kwl. Defo wanna go!	

Name:

Believe me

■ Write a formal letter to your teacher to explain why you were unable to complete a homework project that was due in today.

■ Use the wordbank at the bottom of the page, and your dictionary or thesaurus, to help you choose appropriate vocabulary and to make your teacher believe that you take the homework project seriously.

■ Remember to use the correct letter layout, such as top right-hand side for your address and the date, top left-hand side for your teacher's name and address.

Dear _____

Yours sincerely

_____

apologise	sincerely	assure	dilemma	responsible
disappointed	endeavour	promise	immediately	unavoidable

PHOTOCOPIABLE

SCHOLASTIC
www.scholastic.co.uk

Checking and improving writing

Objective

To proofread for spelling errors and propose changes to vocabulary.

Background knowledge

Children should know how to check their written work and be given opportunities to do so. Proofreading and editing are an integral part of the writing process and should be valued as an opportunity to refine and improve content. Proofreading is also an essential skill for eradicating careless spelling errors. Adequate, allocated time needs to be set aside to make editing, checking and proofing a habit, not a chore to be endured. It is important to highlight the importance of proofreading, not just as a requirement in school but as a life skill. Provide examples of where it is important to carry out checks of written work, such as in journalism, when prescribing medicines, writing laws or judgements and writing reports. It is important, too, that children see you, their teacher, self-editing while modelling writing.

In addition, checking work provides an excellent discussion forum on spelling rules and patterns; it highlights areas needing further work while providing the teacher with useful observations of rules and strategies that are well understood. It also reveals common errors, allowing children to develop individual strategies to improve the quality and accuracy of their writing. Encourage children to check each other's work through writing buddies or partners. Children sometimes learn more from editing a partner's work than they do from editing their own, because they are able to be objective.

Activities

● **Photocopiable page 112 'Editing'**
In this activity the children reinforce their knowledge of the meaning and spelling of words by editing a passage with 21 errors and rewriting them correctly. Before giving copies of the page to the children, read the passage aloud to them and ask them if they understand it. Explain that although it sounds as though it is written correctly, it contains a number of errors that can only be found by reading it rather than listening to it.

● **Photocopiable page 113 'Dull to dynamic'**
Children use their thesauruses to help them come up with more dynamic words than those given. Have a group vote on each table for the best replacement words – provide children with a table showing each dull word followed by a 'winning' column. Once all the winning words have been gathered in, these could form part of the working wall or spelling mobiles.

● **Photocopiable page 114 'Wrong context'**
In this activity, children gain further dictionary practice finding out the meaning of challenging words. It also makes them consider the sense of what they are reading – challenging them to think for themselves which word (or malapropism) is the misfit in each context.

Further ideas

● **Top tips:** Ask the children for a piece of extended writing. Invite them to read through their writing to highlight any spelling errors and make a list of the corrections on the back of the sheet. Have a plenary session where the children discuss the errors and how they identified them. Make a list of the children's top tips for checking work.

● **Add-a-word, change-a-word:** In this self-editing activity, children read through their writing and, where appropriate, insert a word (for example, a powerful adjective) or change a weak word (such as a verb) to a more powerful one. This works well if the writing has been done on alternate lines, as children have more space to make these amendments.

Digital content

On the digital component you will find:
● Printable versions of all three photocopiable pages.
● Answers to all three photocopiable pages.
● Interactive version of 'Editing'.

Name:

Editing

■ Read this passage carefully. There are 21 mistakes (spelling or incorrect use of words). Cross them out and write them correctly at the bottom of the page.

William Shakespeare was a righter of great reknown. He was both a playwrite and poet. He was born in 1564 in a plaice called Stratford-upon-Avon. Later he moved to London to work in the theater. The most famouse theatre was the Globe. It was bilt in a circle with an open roof. Audiences were'nt as well-behaved as they are today. They offen shouted and jeered at the players or through food at the stage. In Elizabethan times, women were not aloud to be acters so boys had to play the femail rolls. Many other aspects of life have changed sins Shakespeare lived. The way people spoke and spelled was diffrent fore hundred years ago so sometimes Shakespeare's language can be trickey to understand. However, because he rote about people and how they behave, his plays are still as poppular today as they where when they were first written.

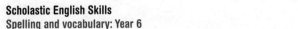

Dull to dynamic

■ It looks like Chloe didn't use a thesaurus to help her come up with more adventurous vocabulary. Replace the dull words in bold with more dynamic words on the adjacent line.

Chloe's homework – description of a garden in summer.

Lots of **nice** _____, **nicely** _____ coloured flowers

were **growing** _____ in the **back** _____ garden.

Yellow _____ buttercups, **blue** _____ hyacinths

and **red** _____ roses **grew along** _____ the

garden's borders, all **next to each other** _____

like spectators at a football match. A **happy** _____ robin

ate _____ **quickly** _____ at the seeds on the bird

table, but flew away when he was **surprised** _____ by the

sight _____ of a **big, orange** _____

cat **walking** _____ across the **soft** _____ grass.

Sunbeams **shone** _____ on the **top** _____ of the

little _____ pond in the corner, making the water

shine _____ and **move** _____.

Name:

Wrong context

■ One word in each of the following sentences is used in the wrong context. The mistaken use of a word in place of a similar-sounding one is called a *malapropism* – often such errors have an amusing effect. Write the correct word on the line below each sentence.

My parents have just started a new hobby; they go flamingo dancing every Saturday morning.

_____

Last year, they tried tantrum bicycling but they soon got tired of that.

_____

Dad's been reading a book about dancing by a unanimous author.

_____

I'm always a bit auspicious when they start something new.

_____

I don't always apprehend why they like different hobbies.

_____

Properly because I am only 11 years old, and I like different things.

_____

Quite honestly, I'm putrefied at the thought of dancing at their age.

_____

I'll definitely come to some other derangement with *my* husband.

_____

In fact, I would be internally grateful if I never got married.

_____

Bringing it all together

To consolidate learning.

Background knowledge

Knowing and being able to spell a wide range of vocabulary is essential to support children's reading and writing. Children can access vocabulary in a variety of ways: through stories, poems, plays, nonfiction and textbooks. It is important that they are given strategies, such as games and interactive activities, to help with their knowledge and understanding and, most of all, to foster an enjoyment of their learning.

The aim of these last three activities is to incorporate some of the key elements of the learning objectives in the book into a range of activities and question types. It is impossible to include spelling and vocabulary from every section, however, and it might be that groups of children – or individuals – require more revision in other areas.

Activities

● **Photocopiable page 116 'More prefixes and suffixes'**
This activity requires the children to further demonstrate their knowledge and understanding of adding prefixes and suffixes to root words, either to create antonyms or to transform adjectives into verbs. It may be necessary to provide children with a dictionary to support them with the 'Challenge' section at the bottom of the page.

● **Photocopiable page 117 'Spelling rules and synonyms'**
In this activity, children consolidate their understanding of the ambiguity between words with a hyphenated prefix and those where the prefix is joined to the root word. They also need to show that they remember the *i before e* spelling rule. The final part of the activity is to match given words to their synonyms.

● **Photocopiable page 118 'Know your words'**
In this activity, children hunt for spelling errors. The misspelled words are all linked to previous sections of the book – for example, adding 'ible' or 'able' to root words (*impossible*) or words with silent letters (*Wednesday*). Finally, children will need to demonstrate their understanding of pairs of homophones by writing them in context, in sentences.

Further ideas

● **Guided reading:** Continue to discuss the spelling of tricky words as you come across them with the children. Ask them to share with you and their fellow learners the strategies that they use to help them. Discuss as a group why some strategies are better than others and who feels they are a visual, kinaesthetic or audio learner.
● **Make a game:** Give different groups of children – or pairs – a spelling topic for which they must create a game. For example, the negative prefixes 'dis', 'mis', 'un', 'il' and 'ir'. Discuss games they are already familiar with, such as Snakes and Ladders, and how these might be adapted to reinforce spelling patterns and rules.

Digital content

On the digital component you will find:
- Printable versions of all three photocopiable pages.
- Answers to all three photocopiable pages.
- Interactive versions of 'More prefixes and suffixes' and 'Spelling rules and synonyms'.

Name:

Bringing it all together

More prefixes and suffixes

■ Add a prefix to the beginning of each word to form its antonym.

_____appropriate   _____perfect

_____mortal   _____replaceable

_____legal

■ Add each of these suffixes to the end of the root words, making any necessary spelling adjustments.

Root word	ence	ed
prefer		
infer		
refer		

■ Add the appropriate suffix to turn these adjectives into verbs. Write the new words on the lines.

intense   _____

solid   _____

pure   _____

clear   _____

Challenge:

brief _____

captive _____

authoritative _____

Bringing it all together

Spelling rules and synonyms

Hyphenated words
■ Draw a line to match the definition to the correct word.

to feel well again	re-form
to act or speak for someone	re-present
to offer something again	reform
to make something again	re-cover
to put a new layer on something	recover
to improve something/someone	represent

i before e
■ Circle the correctly spelled word in the following sentences.

The presents were gratefully **received/recieved** by the children.

Both climbers succeeded in climbing the **glaceir/glacier**.

My dog gave me a **weird/wierd** look when I suggested a walk in the rain.

Synonyms
■ Match the words in bold to their correct synonyms.

I **frequently** forget to wear my hat.	fearless
The ship was on the right **course** for America.	spellbound
The prince was **mesmerised** by the princess's beauty.	track
The **intrepid** explorer made camp close to the elephants.	very often

Name:

Know your words

Check it!

■ There are 20 spelling errors in the following text. Cross them out and write them correctly in the box below.

My best freind, Joe, was really impossable to predict; one minute he liked serial for breakfast, the next he prefered toast. I guest that he was probibly capible of eating either won but it depended witch sighed of the bed he got out of. Joe was an incredably kind buoy who recieved a lot of prays from teachers and children alike. Last Wensday, he had a bad coff; althow he's a tuff lad, he was incredably week after a couple of days of virtually no food.

■ Write a sentence for each of the following homophones, to show you know the difference in their meanings.

affect _____

effect _____

principle _____

principal _____

alter _____

altar _____

Assessment

Assessment grid

The following grid shows the main objectives and activities covered in this chapter. You can use the grid to locate activities that cover a particular focus that you are keen to monitor.

Objective	Page	Activity title
To use a dictionary to check the spelling and meaning of words.	96 97 98	Dictionary work Get to the root What sort of word?
To know how words are related by meaning as synonyms and antonyms.	100 101 102 117	Synonyms and antonyms Notes in class Antonyms and opposites Spelling rules and synonyms
To use a thesaurus.	104 105 106	The Lion and the Mouse Adventurous adjectives and astounding adverbs Wise words
To understand the difference between vocabulary typical of informal speech and vocabulary appropriate for formal speech and writing.	108 109 110	Can I join you? Text translation Believe me
To proofread for spelling errors.	112 113 114 118	Editing Dull to dynamic Wrong context Know your words
To use further prefixes and suffixes.	116	More prefixes and suffixes

Observation and record keeping

While the children are completing the photocopiable sheets in this chapter, find opportunities to observe them as they work and discuss reasons for vocabulary choices – prompting them to make more adventurous choices. Make notes of outcomes against a class list. Encourage the children to keep a word bank to record vocabulary they have found interesting, unusual or difficult. Encourage the children to share their completed photocopiable sheets and word banks with a partner and to discuss their vocabulary choices, successes and difficulties. Keep the children's photocopiable sheets as a record of vocabulary-enrichment activities.

Assessment activity

- **What you need**
Photocopiable page 120 'Synonym and antonym'.
- **What to do**
In this assessment activity, children choose a synonym or antonym that is the closest match for specific words, some of which appear in a sentence. This will demonstrate both their understanding of synonyms and antonyms and their ability to show nuances of meaning.

Differentiation

- For less confident learners, ask them to explain their choice verbally.
- Ask more confident learners to add another synonym or antonym from their own knowledge that could be used as a substitute for the adjective in each sentence.

Further learning

- **Quick-fire activities:** Hold short, quick-fire activities at the beginning or end of the day or lesson. Say an adjective or adverb aloud and ask the children to call out a synonym as an instant response. Have a similar session using antonyms. Begin with simple vocabulary, such as *hot* and *cold*, gradually increasing the difficulty. Vary the activity by using the word in a phrase or sentence to encourage the children to think about its context.
- **Subject-specific vocabulary:** Challenge children in their writing, particularly non-fiction, to use subject-specific vocabulary to set their subject in context. For example, in an information text about climbing Mount Everest, give them a word bank to refer to with words such as *crampons*, *ice axe*, *carabiners* or *oxygen*.

Name:

Assessment

Synonym and antonym

■ Write synonyms for the following words, taking note of the word class of each word. Use a dictionary if you need help.

to compliment (verb) _____ a compliment (noun) _____

to influence (verb) _____ an influence (noun) _____

to answer (verb) _____ an answer (noun) _____

to hug (verb) _____ a hug (noun) _____

to attack (verb) _____ an attack (noun) _____

■ Choose **one** verb to replace each verb and adverb highlighted in **bold**.

I felt **really tired** _____ so I sat down for a rest. Meanwhile, my new

puppy, the cause of my tiredness, was **running quickly** _____ around

the garden! I thought he would **have laid down exhaustedly** _____

himself by now but that clearly wasn't going to happen. After I told him off for

completely ruining _____ Mum's flowerbed extravaganza (goodness

only knows how **terribly cross** _____ she would be), he **quietly**

walked _____ off to a corner and **soon fell asleep** _____

for about five minutes. Before I knew it, he was **running madly** _____

across the garden towards me again!

■ Rewrite these sentences, replacing the words in **bold** with a suitable antonym. You may need to make further changes to the sentence so that it makes sense.

My brother's friend is really **aggressive**. He always helps me with my homework and **discourages** me from working hard.

_____

_____

After school has **started**, we all go to the park for a **stressful** play on the swings. If the weather is **foul**, we lie in the sun and chatter **miserably** about our summer holidays.

_____

_____

PHOTOCOPIABLE ■SCHOLASTIC www.scholastic.co.uk

Glossary

adjective: Adjectives can be used before a noun, to make the noun's meaning more specific (to modify the noun), or after the verb 'to be', as its complement. Adjectives cannot be modified by other adjectives. This distinguishes them from nouns, which can be.

adverb: Adverbs can modify a verb, an adjective, another adverb or even a whole clause. While it is true that many adverbs end in 'ly', this is not universally true (*soon* or *very*).

ambiguity: Having more than one interpretation or meaning.

antonym: A word opposite in meaning to another.

apostrophe: Apostrophes show either missing letters (contractions), such as *don't*, or possession, such as *Tom's book*. In singular nouns, apostrophes showing possession are placed *before* the 's' (*cat's*), in regular plural nouns they are placed *after* the 's' (*cats'*), but irregular plural nouns they come before 's' (*children's*).

compound word: Two words that are joined to make one longer word, such as *bad-tempered, bedroom*.

consonant: The 21 letters of the alphabet that are not vowels ('a', 'e', 'i', 'o', 'u').

etymology: The study of the origin of words and how they have changed over time.

grapheme: A letter or a number of letters that represent a sound (phoneme) in a word.

GPC: Grapheme–phoneme correspondence – the relationship between sounds and the letters that represent those sounds.

homophone: A word that sounds the same as another word but has a different meaning and is spelled differently. Near-homophones are words that sound almost the same and are often confused (such as *accept/except, affect/effect*).

hyphen: A punctuation mark used to join words (*co-production* and *first-hand)*.

letter string: A sequence of letters that occurs frequently, such as 'ough'.

malapropism: The mistaken use of a word in place of a similar-sounding one.

morphology: The internal make-up of a word in terms of root words, suffixes and prefixes, as well as other changes (such as *mouse* to *mice*).

noun: Nouns are naming words for people, places, animals and things. They can also name abstract ideas that cannot be seen or touched, such as *courage* or *love*.

phoneme: The smallest unit of sound in speech.

possessive word: Words that show ownership. They may use the apostrophe in singular or plural forms (*the boy's book* or *the boys' books*), or be possessive pronouns such as *mine, yours*.

prefix: A prefix is added to the beginning of a word to make another word (such as *regular* becoming *irregular*).

root word: A word that can stand alone but have prefixes or suffixes added to modify it, such as *form* becoming *inform/formation/forming*.

silent letter: A letter that may once have been pronounced or sounded but no longer is (such as the 'k' in *knight*).

stressed and unstressed syllables: A stressed syllable is one that is emphasised. For example, in the word *reference*, the first syllable, 'ref', is stressed or emphasised, whereas the second two syllables ('er' and 'ence') are unstressed and not emphasised.

suffix: Suffixes are added at the end of root words to change them into another word, such as *office* to *official*. Sometimes the addition of a suffix changes the spelling of the root word (*wary* to *warily*). A suffix cannot stand alone.

syllable: Words consist of one or more syllables. They are like the beats of a word and can be counted (*word* has one syllable, *sentence* has two). Syllables have at least one vowel and possibly one or more consonants.

synonym: A word with the same or similar meaning as another.

verb: Verbs describe actions, states of being or feelings.

word class: The four main word classes in the English language are: nouns, adjectives, adverbs and verbs.

word family: Groups of words that are related closely enough to each other to form a 'family'.

Word bank

Prefixes

Basic	Intermediate	Advanced
disagree	disconnect	disadvantage
disapprove	disregard	discourage
mistake	misjudge	misapprehend
misunderstand	misplace	miscalculate
recover	reconsider	readdress
rewrite	unravel	reapply
unload	unbalance	reassemble

Suffixes – adjectives and adverbs

Basic	Intermediate	Advanced
bearable – bearably	acceptable – acceptably	abominable – abominably
believable – believably	admirable – admirably	deniable – deniably
horrible – horribly	audible – audibly	indescribable – indescribably
responsible – responsibly	changeable – changeably	legible – legibly
sensible – sensibly	reversible – reversibly	plausible – plausibly
terrible – terribly	visible – visibly	reprehensible – reprehensibly

Suffixes – converting nouns and adjectives into verbs

Basic	Intermediate	Advanced
advert – advertise	abbreviation – abbreviate	amplification – amplify
class – classify	association – associate	economy – economise
hard – harden	donation – donate	glory – glorify
length – lengthen	qualification – qualify	intense – intensify
pure – purify	reality – realise	quantity – quantify
soft – soften	solid – solidify	speciality – specialise

Hyphenated words

Basic	Intermediate	Advanced
bad-tempered	ill-advised	accident-prone
dark-eyed	re-act	co-own
fair-skinned	re-call	pre-arrange
kind-hearted	re-establish	re-cover
quick-thinking	self-assessment	re-present

Spelling patterns – 'ough' letter string   Chapter 3

Basic	Intermediate	Advanced
enough rough tough	brought ought cough trough nought	borough bough thorough

Silent letters

Basic	Intermediate	Advanced
cupboard knight gnome knot handsome limb honest scratch hour thumb	castle subtle descend Wednesday foreign whistle island wrinkle reign wrist	aisle psychology heir rhythm isle rhombus isosceles scissors pnuemonia wrangle

Homophones and near homophones   Chapter 5

Basic	Intermediate	Advanced
been/bean stare/stair fair/fare to/two/too hair/hare tire/tyre see/sea there/they're/their	advice/advise seen/scene affect/effect serial/cereal cord/chord toad/towed paws/pause write/right/rite	complementary/ licence/license complimentary practice/practise foul/fowl principle/principal licence/license raise/raze

Synonyms

Basic	Intermediate	Advanced
annoying disappointed marvellous serious smell	irritating downcast breathtaking/spectacular grave scent/whiff/pong	exasperating/infuriating dispirited/despondent sensational sombre stench

Antonyms

Basic	Intermediate	Advanced
load/unload steady/unsteady regular/irregular	appropriate/inappropriate legible/illegible advantage/disadvantage	mortal/immortal service/disservice sincere/insincere

General activities

How to use the general activities

These activities can be used in a flexible way to support your teaching of spelling and vocabulary. They include a variety of games and activities for use in groups or as whole-class activities, all of which can be generic ways of exploring the work covered in each of the chapters in the book. You may choose to use these games and activities as part of your spelling routine, mental warm-ups, plenaries or as part of your main lesson. They are designed to be fast-paced activities, used to reinforce or assess spellings. The five-minute ideas on page 127 can be used as warm-ups or plenaries.

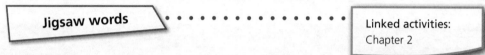

Jigsaw words

Linked activities:
Chapter 2

What to do

● Give the children a list of words with prefixes, suffixes and roots separated, such as *in-describe-ably*. Ask them to cut the words up so that the root word and the prefixes/suffixes are separated like jigsaw pieces. Mix up the pieces and invite the children to race each other at putting the words back together, ensuring that any changes to the root word spelling are made. Children can either write the full word on a whiteboard or mark any spelling changes on the cut-out card.
● Adapt this to include words with suffixes such as 'cious', 'tious', 'cial', 'tial', 'ency', 'ence', 'ancy' and 'ance'.

What's the word?

Linked activities:
any spellings in the book

What to do

● Use this activity to focus on a target set of words that the children are aware of.
● Organise the class into two teams, with half the class in each.
● Groups will choose a different person to represent them for each round of the game. The children representing their groups must stand.
● Each group gets to observe the other group in action.
● Give each representative (or 'teacher') a word on a piece of paper that the others cannot see. Without showing the word to anyone, or spelling the word, they must describe the word to their group using clues like 'it has a prefix', 'it has three syllables', 'it is a noun', 'it is an opposite' or 'it sounds like…'. The group can also ask yes/no questions such as 'Does it have five letters?' or 'Is the prefix 'un'?'. The 'teacher' can only answer 'yes' or 'no'.
● Each group has a time limit (three minutes) to work out the word. At the end of the time, the 'teacher' must write the word on the board for everyone to see. If the group guessed it, they get a point.
● The winning group is the group with the most points.

Syllable race

Linked activities:
Chapter 5

What to do

● Arrange the children into small, mixed-ability teams around each table. Appoint a secretary for each team.

● Write a syllable on the board. Each member of each team writes as many words as possible containing that syllable on their own whiteboard within a limited timeframe.

● When the time is up, the teams should count up the total number of words that the whole group has written and spelled correctly. Any duplicate words only count once.

● Each team secretary should then write the team list on a whiteboard and hold it up for all the other teams to see.

● Other teams can challenge words; if they are incorrect, they must be wiped off the list.

● The team that has written the most correct words within the timeframe wins.

● Extend the game by writing a letter string or suffix on the board, rather than a syllable. For example, the teams write as many words containing the suffix 'cious' as they can within the timeframe.

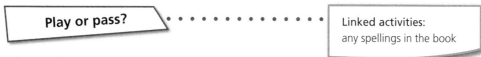

Play or pass?

Linked activities:
any spellings in the book

What to do

● Select a number of words you want the children to revise or that they frequently spell incorrectly.

● Choose an appropriate number of words so that there are at least two words for each child in the group.

● Arrange the children in a circle.

● Ask the first child (child 1) in the circle to spell a particular word. The child can choose to play or pass. If child 1 chooses to play, they must spell the word correctly to get a point. If child 1 chooses to pass, they pass the word to the child next to them (child 2). Child 2 must then attempt to spell the word – the word can no longer be passed. If child 2 spells it correctly, they win the point. If child 2 spells it incorrectly, the point is awarded to child 1.

● Now ask child 2 to spell a new word. Child 2 can now choose to play or pass. If child 2 chooses to pass, child 3 must attempt the word. If child 2 chooses to play and spells the word correctly, child 2 wins the point. Then ask child 3 to spell a new word.

● Continue around the group until all the words you have chosen have been spelled.

Spell a word

Linked activities:
all chapters

What to do

● Provide the children with a list of words, letter tiles (with values per letter) and boards with grids on them (include special squares, such as five bonus points).

● Tell them to spell out each word using the letter tiles and work out their numerical values, for example, *extreme* might have a value of 16, but a longer word, *delicious* only has a value of 12.

● Ask the children to work in small groups. Tell each group to arrange the words from the list on the board in the fashion of a crossword. Using the special squares, each group tries to get the highest total score for the word list.

Spelling relay

Linked activities:
all chapters

What to do

● Prepare three lists of words with different levels of challenge, give them headings (A, B or C). Write them on a board or pin them to a wall. Allocate points for each word list according to the challenge, for example, 'A' words are worth 2 points, 'B' words are worth 4 points and 'C' words are worth 10 points.

● Arrange the children into two mixed teams in two lines facing the board. Allow them a few minutes to become familiar with the words on the board.

● The first child from each team (the speller) stands with their back to the board so that they cannot see the word lists. The next child from each team asks this child to choose a list, A, B or C, and asks them to spell one word from it. If it is spelled correctly, the team wins the points, the word is crossed out and the speller joins the team at the back of the line. If the child gets it wrong, there is no score.

● The next child now at the front becomes the speller and stands at the front facing the team. Continue until all the words have been crossed out.

● The team with the highest score is the winner.

● To vary this game, give each team one list only that consists of the same words of mixed difficulty. The teams must spell the words on the list and cross out the words when spelled correctly. The winning team is the first team to cross out all the words on their list.

Yes or no game

Linked activities:
any spellings in the book

What to do

● Tell the children you have written a secret word on a sticky note (which you stick, back to front, on the board to increase suspense).

● The children must ask you questions, in the manner of the 'Yes and No' game, to try to ascertain what the word is. You can only answer 'yes' or 'no'!

● Question types: word class, does it have a prefix/suffix, is it in the plural (if noun), if a verb then what person/tense, how many letters and so on.

● Variations: put a cap on the number of questions they are allowed to ask. This will prevent 'silly' or unhelpful questions.

● Put a word bank on the board and tell the children the word has been selected from the bank – this will make it easier.

● Children could do this activity in ability groups, where you give a nominated 'teacher' the word in advance.

What's my word?

Linked activities:
Chapters 1 and 2

What to do

● Select a list of words you want the children to revise. Display the word list.

● Ask the children to choose one word from the list. Tell them to investigate their chosen word by taking it apart and putting it back together again.

● Invite them to write the word on their whiteboards. Ask them to say the word out loud and count the syllables. Tell them to underline the syllables on their whiteboards.

● Next, count the phonemes and write the number next to the word.

● Then tell them to look for prefixes, suffixes and root words. Encourage them to look for spelling rules and mnemonics that apply to their chosen word and any other features, for example, double consonants, digraphs, silent letters, word origins and meaning.

● When they have had sufficient time to investigate the word thoroughly, tell them to write their findings in no more than two sentences on a strip of paper and erase their whiteboards. The sentences are to act as a clue to the word.

● Ask the children to take turns to come to the front and read out their clues. The rest of the children try to work out what the word is and write it down and hold up their whiteboards.

Five-minute ideas

Spelling A B C
● Choose a word and write it in alphabetical order on the board, for example, 'underneath' becomes 'adeehnnrtu'. Ask the children to make as many words as they can, like this, in a limited time. Give them points for the most words and bonus points if anyone finds the whole original word.

Newspaper spelling
● Arrange the children into groups of three. Provide them with sheets of newspaper. Call out a word and the children have to tear out letters and put them together to make the word. The group that succeeds and spells it correctly first wins.

Back to back spelling
● Arrange the children so that they are standing in a circle. Choose someone and tell them to use a finger to write a word on their neighbour's back. The neighbour must then say the word aloud. If they get it wrong they drops out and the first one has another turn. If they get it right he then writes on the next child's back and so on.

Missing letter race
● Arrange the children in groups, give each child a number and provide each group with a set of magnetic letters. Write a word on a magnetic board with one letter missing. The groups find the missing magnetic letter and child 1 from each group tries to be the first to put it into place. Write another word on the board and miss out two letters. Children 2 and 3 from each group try to be the first to put them into place. Continue until you finish with a word that has only one letter written on the board. To avoid children bumping into each other, place a marker before the board and the first child to reach it is allowed to put the letter on the board.

Find my family
● Prepare a set of root words, prefix and suffix cards. Divide the root cards between four or five children. Give the remaining children a prefix or suffix card. Ask a root card holder to stand at the front and the rest of the children read their cards. If they can make a word in the same family they come and join the root. Each one should say and spell their word.

Spelling consequences
● Arrange the children into groups of five or six. Give each of the groups a strip of paper. Choose one child in each group to begin. Ask them to think of a word with the same number of letters as group members, without telling the group what it is, and write the first letter on the strip of paper. The strip is then passed around with each child adding a letter that could follow the letter(s) already written. When they have all had a turn, ask the first child to say the word they had thought of and read the word on the completed strip.

● As a variation, give the children a strip of paper with a three letter word written on it and fold over the first letter. The strip is passed around the group and each group member looks at the two showing letters and adds a letter to the word. When everyone has had a turn, they read their result. Is it a real word or a nonsense word?